THE QUEEN'S DOMAIN

ADVANCING GOD'S KINGDOM
IN THE 40/70 WINDOW

THE QUEEN'S DOMAIN

ADVANCING GOD'S KINGDOM
IN THE 40/70 WINDOW

C. PETER WAGNER, EDITOR

The Queen's Domain
Copyright © 2000
by C. Peter Wagner
ISBN 1-58502-009-5

Published by
Wagner Publications
11005 N. Highway 83
Colorado Springs, CO 80921
www.wagnerpublications.org

Cover design by
Erin Mathis
emdesign Studio
1035 Tehama Avenue
Menlo Park, CA 94025
www.emdesignstudio.com

Edit and Interior design by
Rebecca Sytsema

Rights for publishing this book in other languages are contracted by Gospel Literature International (GLINT). GLINT also provides technical help for the adaptation, translation, and publishing of Bible study resources and books in scores of languages worldwide. For further information, contact GLINT, P.O. Box 4060, Ontario, CA 91761-1003, USA. You may also send e-mail to glintint@aol.com, or visit their web site at www.glint.org.

1 2 3 4 5 6 7 8 9   06 05 04 03 02 01 00

TABLE OF CONTENTS

CHAPTER ONE

THE POWER OF
STRATEGIC INTERCESSION

by C. Peter Wagner

The most awesome initiative involving strategic intercession that I am aware of took place over a two-year period
in what was called "Operation Queen's Palace." The vision
for that remarkable spiritual outreach began to take shape in
Ephesus, Turkey, in August 1997 and the various prayer activities that ensued ended in October 1999 with "Celebration
Ephesus," a four-hour prayer and praise event, and the "Praying Through the Window IV" prayer campaign of the
A.D.2000 United Prayer Track. I will provide a bit more
detail on these prayer efforts later on, but first of all I want to
explain this book's title: *The Queen's Domain.*

The Queen's Domain

My earlier book, *Confronting the Queen of Heaven* (Wagner
Publications), gives the entire background leading up to Operation Queen's Palace and Celebration Ephesus. The

"Queen" we are referring to is the Queen of Heaven, one of the most insidious members of Satan's hierarchy of darkness. *Confronting the Queen of Heaven* contains the information that led me to a quite radical conclusion: *"[The Queen of Heaven] is the demonic principality who is most responsible under Satan for keeping unbelievers in spiritual darkness"* (p. 17).

The ongoing research that we have been able to do on the Queen of Heaven since beginning Operation Queen's Palace has served to substantiate this hypothesis more and more. Among other things, we have concluded that one of the physical power points from which the Queen of Heaven radiates her power of evil, perhaps even her central earthly power point, is Ephesus, Turkey. We, therefore, saw Ephesus as a "palace" of this queen, and that is why we called our two-year strategic prayer initiative "Operation Queen's Palace."

The 40/70 Window

Now it has become evident that the area of the world in which the Queen of Heaven, in all probability, exercises more unchallenged control than in any other large area is the 40/70 Window, stretching between 40° and 70° north latitude from Iceland in the west to the tip of Siberia in the east.

We have chosen to call the 40/70 Window "Queen's Domain" because we believe that she is keeping a larger percentage of the population blinded to the gospel of Jesus Christ in this particular region than in any other similar area of the world. Her two main disguises appear to be: (1) a counterfeit Mary in populations that were once Christian and (2) the Moon Goddess in populations that are Muslim, such as the ancient Silk Road.

The Queen's Domain: 40/70 Window

This book, *The Queen's Domain: Advancing God's Kingdom in the 40/70 Window*, is a challenge for some Christians—certainly not the whole Body of Christ—to join us in a strategic intercession initiative at least as large, and perhaps larger than Operation Queen's Palace, which we are calling "Operation Queen's Domain."

Warfare Is Not for Everyone

I realize that I have been using the term "strategic intercession" frequently without explaining what I mean by it. Let me say at the outset that this book is not an entry-level book on spiritual warfare. It is very advanced. That is why I just said that it is not for the whole Body of Christ. When God gave the first law of warfare to His people in Deuteronomy 20, He clearly told them that warfare was not for everyone. Those who had built a new house or those who had just planted vineyards or those who were newlyweds or those who were fearful or fainthearted were excused with no penalty (see Deut. 20:5-8). God had chosen only a few for the battle. Of the 32,000 who were with Gideon, God chose only 300 to defeat the Midianites (see Judges 7:2-6).

God is doing a similar thing today. He is choosing a few for battle, not because they are bigger or stronger or quicker or smarter or better looking or more precious to Him than anyone else in the Body of Christ. He is choosing them, like He chose improbable individuals such as an Abraham or a Moses or an Esther or a David, simply because He has decided that they are individuals whom He desires to anoint and empower for a specific task in His kingdom in this hour. They will have a compassion for the lost, they will understand the inner workings of the invisible world, they will have gifts of intercession and prophecy, they will be holy, they will have unconditional obedience to God, and they will not love their lives to the death.

Strategic Intercession Focuses on the Lost

God once chose 300 such people to defeat the Midianites. Our warfare today, however, is not against flesh and blood, but against principalities and powers and rulers of the darkness of this age (see Eph. 6:12). Victory in this present-day war will come as multitudes of lost people are taken from the power of Satan to God (see Acts 26:18).

The underlying purpose of Operation Queen's Domain is effective evangelism. The biblical reason that more people are not being saved is because the god of this age has their minds blinded to the gospel (see 2 Cor. 4:3-4). God does not want any of them to perish in hell. His word to us is that "You shall receive power when the Holy Spirit has come upon you, and you shall be witnesses to Me in Jerusalem, and in all Judea, and Samaria, (and the 40/70 Window)," if I may be allowed a bit of liberty with the text (see Acts 1:8). It is the people of God who are to implement the evangelization of the world.

No responsible general sends the ground troops into battle without first controlling the air. To reverse the procedure would be suicide. But in our evangelism we have often been guilty of that very thing. We send missionaries and evangelists and church planters and pastors out to the unreached peoples and wonder why they often return home battered and bruised and discouraged. It is because the prince of the power of the air still controls the territory. Our job is to displace him so that the light of the gospel can shine, and our principal weapon for doing that is strategic intercession.

Three Levels of Spiritual Warfare

Those who have followed the development of the worldwide prayer movement of the 1990s know that the International Spiritual Warfare Network has determined that it is helpful to distinguish three levels of spiritual warfare:

♦ **Ground-level spiritual warfare** involves casting demons out of individuals.

♦ **Occult-level spiritual warfare** means confronting more organized forms of demonic power such as we might find in witchcraft, Satanism, Santería, Freemasonry, Eastern religions, and various other forms of the occult.

♦ **Strategic-level spiritual warfare** undertakes confronting the high-ranking principalities and powers that wield ungodly control over territories such as cities or nations or people groups or other social networks.

The term "strategic intercession" places prayer activities like Operation Queen's Domain mostly in the category of strategic-level spiritual warfare. It is important to keep in mind, however, that the world of darkness is one world in which whatever is done on any one of the three levels has its ripple effect on the other two. Those strategic intercessors whom God calls to participate on the front lines of Operation Queen's Domain will, therefore, find themselves involved with all three levels of spiritual warfare. But the main focus will remain strategic-level warfare.

Prophetic Intercession

Let's add another adjective, "prophetic," when we think of strategic intercession. Before the prayer movement of the 1990s, few people were talking about "prophetic intercession," but now the term and the practice is much more common. In fact, Barbara Wentroble has just written an entire book called *Prophetic Intercession.* She says, "In prophetic intercession, we come into the presence of the Lord and hear His mind and counsel. We are then able to pray things that are on His heart. Too often we pray the things that are on our hearts and fail to hear Him. It is through seeking, hearing, and speaking forth His mind that we see powerful breakthrough occur."[1]

Prophetic intercession, as we understand it for Operation Queen's Domain, may involve some outward behavior that predictably would seem strange to many Christians. For example, some of Barbara Wentroble's headings include "Dancing, Shouting and Clapping," "Prayerwalking," "Prophetic Music," "Prophetic Proclamations," "Strategic Declarations," "Spiritual Shouts," and other rather unconventional actions that few have seen in their church's Wednesday evening prayer meeting.

Prophetic Acts

Through the 1990s those of us in the worldwide prayer movement learned a great deal about the power of prophetic acts. In the process we have seen our share of flakiness, some of which has turned certain individuals against the practice of prophetic acts in general. One encouraging thing that I have observed, however, is that, if I am not mistaken, we see considerably less flakiness now than we did, say, ten years ago. I have yet to meet an intercessor who wants to be flaky, and most of them are ready and willing to learn how to improve.

Barbara Wentroble defines a prophetic act as, "A thing or deed done, having the powers of a prophet; an action or decree that predicts or foreshadows."[2] Here is Dutch Sheets' definition: "Prophetic action or declaration is something said or done in the natural realm at the direction of God that prepares the way for Him to move in the spiritual realm."[3]

We could remind ourselves of biblical prophetic acts such as Jeremiah burying his underwear for a time (see Jeremiah 13) or Isaiah walking around naked (see Isaiah 20) or Joshua's troops walking around a city seven times and blowing horns (see Joshua 6).

Eagles of God

As I am writing this we are planning to send our first prophetic, strategic intercession team of what we call "Eagles of God" into the 40/70 Window and around the world in connection with Operation Queen's Domain. Chuck Pierce, who has a later chapter in this book on the subject, feels that Operation Queen's Domain is destined to open incredible storehouses of financial resources for world evangelization. As the leader of this seven-member prayer team, Chuck had called a strategizing session in the World Prayer Center. Just before the session, one of Chuck's intercessors wrote and said that, as she was praying for him, she heard God (prophetic intercession!) say that the team was to bury a gold coin in each city that they had earmarked for prayer. As he shared it with the group, my wife, Doris, mentioned that in our last conference someone had donated a bag of small gold coins and that she hadn't sold them as yet. They were all elated. They counted the cities, which were ten. Then Doris brought in the bag of coins, laid them on the table, and there were exactly ten! As frosting on the cake, they were 1/10th oz. coins, each one of them imprinted with an *eagle*!

Not too many other people are planning on going around the world this year and burying gold coins in ten cities. But these Eagles of God are, purely and simply in obedience to God. This is a classic example of prophetic intercession and a prophetic act which has world-changing potential.

Fresh Examples
of Strategic Intercession

There were many outstanding prayer initiatives during the extraordinary decade of the 1990s. I think of the four Praying Through the Window projects each of which mobilized from 20 million to 40 million intercessors praying for the same thing on the same day through a whole month. I think of the Day to Change the World in 1994 with the first International March for Jesus. I think of the annual praying through Ramadan efforts called "Muslim Prayer Focus." I think of the 1993 Gideon's Army meeting in Korea, the 1,937 Bethany Unreached People Group Profiles, the dedication of the World Prayer Center in Colorado Springs, and many other happenings.

But I have selected four prayer actions which, more than some of the others, will help us understand strategic intercession, prophetic acts, and Operation Queen's Domain.

Cardinal Points Prayer
1991 & 1994

When Roger McKnight, who was affiliated with Youth With a Mission (YWAM) in Australia, first heard that we had scheduled the Day to Change the World for June 25, 1994, he remembered a "Cardinal Points Prayer Strategy" that YWAM had experimented with in 1991. They had researched the geographically extreme points of six continents, north, south, east, and west, and they had dispatched a team of strategic intercessors to all 24 points to pray the same day. Even though it was a formidable challenge to reach a number of the 24 places, they were able to do it.

In 1994 the AD2000 United Prayer Track became involved and it expanded to cover not only the 24 continental cardinal points, but also the cardinal points of as many *nations* as possible. We have never been able to compile a total report, but we do know that Harold Caballeros of Guatemala, our Latin American Coordinator, did an amazing job. He mapped out the cardinal points of Central America, South America, each Latin American nation, and Guatemala City where he lives. He had metal stakes manufactured and specially inscribed for each of the cardinal points. Not only did the strategic intercessors reach all of the cardinal points, but as they prayed they also did a prophetic act of driving the stake into the ground, claiming that area for the Kingdom of God.

The Reconciliation Walk
1996-1999

The power of identificational repentance in strategic intercession became known during the 1990s through John Dawson and others. Some prayer leaders in England such as John Presdee had modeled the concept of prayer expeditions with teams of strategic intercessors mapping the route from London to Berlin, for example, and walking the distance, praying strategically as they were walking.

Lynn Green of Youth With a Mission combined these ideas and launched the Body of Christ on the most massive example we have to date of a prophetic act centered on identificational repentance. He and his team mapped out all the known routes of the First Crusade from Cologne, Germany, to Jerusalem. Then, on the 900th anniversary of the First Crusade, which spanned 1096 to 1099, hundreds of intercessors walked those routes for three years with one agenda item: public repentance for the sins of our Christian ancestors against the Muslims and Jews of the area. Their magnificent entrance into Jerusalem on July 15, 1999, was one of the highlights of the Christian history of the decade.

Operation Ice Castle
1997

Ana Méndez, the Spiritual Warfare Network coordinator for Southern Mexico, had been leading intercessors in fervent prayer for the 10/40 Window, to the extent of establishing a 10/40 Window prayer tower in Mexico City. One day in her tower the Lord showed her that a major stronghold of darkness for the whole 10/40 Window was on Mt. Everest in the Himalaya Mountains. She had a vision of the Himalayas like a huge castle of ice, so we named the expedition, "Operation Ice Castle." This was also the first direct assault on the Queen of Heaven. The original name of Mt. Everest in Nepali is

Sagarmatha, meaning "Mother of the Universe!"

In September 1997 a team of 24 strategic intercessors were deployed in Nepal. A group led by my wife, Doris, prayed for three weeks in a hotel with no hot water at 13,000 feet. Others prayed at the Everest Base Camp at 18,000 feet. Ana, and a team that had taken Alpine training with her, crossed bottomless crevasses and scaled the mountain to 20,000 feet where they did a series of prophetic acts at what they perceived to be the physical power point of the Queen of Heaven. This involved such physical, emotional, and spiritual risks that we kept the strategic expedition a secret until all were safely home.

Operation Queen's Palace 1997-1999

The climax of the strategic intercession events of the decade was Operation Queen's Palace, which I mentioned at the beginning of this chapter. When Doris and I visited Turkey for the first time in 1997 we each received a different prophetic word from the Lord. Doris sensed that the power of Diana of the Ephesians was still there, although in another form. I saw the ancient amphitheater where Paul had experienced the riot dedicated to Diana (see Acts 19) filled with Christians praising Jesus of Nazareth. Thus, Operation Queen's Palace was birthed.

For two years we mobilized the International Spiritual Warfare Network in a frontal attack on the Queen of Heaven. We published the book, *Confronting the Queen of Heaven* (Wagner Publications). Spiritual mappers in many nations located the principal power points for the different disguises that the Queen was using. Numerous prayer exercises combined with prophetic acts were done, but the heaviest concentration of them all came in August and September 1999.

A major solar eclipse took place on a strip 70 miles wide and 8,700 miles long from England to India, with Turkey as the mid point. Intercessors heard prophetically that this would be a concentrated effort on the part of the occult practitioners of the world to increase their evil power. The *Denver Post* said, "The heavens will stage their culminating spectacle when the last solar eclipse of the millennium streaks through Europe and the Middle East." New agers, witches, warlocks, shamans, wizards, mediums, and the like had virtually all hotels booked solid along the path of the eclipse.

The Spiritual Warfare Network, meanwhile, had given green-beret training to 17 teams of strategic intercessors, called "Lions," who were deployed along the path of the eclipse. In England 18 similar teams had been trained under Roger Mitchell, for a total of 35 teams. Strategic intercession and prophetic acts were helping to neutralize any occult power that was being called down from the realm of darkness. Among other things, it was reported that a popular Romanian witch cancelled her participation in the eclipse ceremonies because the spirits she had been in communication with no longer were responding to her!

Celebration Ephesus

Our October 1, 1999 finale, "Celebration Ephesus," was a magnificent event from every conceivable perspective. Some 5,000 individuals from 62 nations gathered in the amphitheater in ancient Ephesus, Turkey, to lift praises and prayers and worship and Scripture declarations and honor to the Lord for four hours non-stop. It closed with a magnificent rendering of Handel's "Hallelujah Chorus" by the 100-voice Kwang Lim Methodist Korean Choir. The Holy Spirit visited us with an anointing of compassion and generosity and we were able to leave over $75,000 US for the Turkish Protestant Earthquake Relief Committee.

The intensity of strategic intercession during the decade of the 1990s had never been seen previously in the history of the church. But, did it pay off? I want to look at the answer to that question in the next chapter.

Notes

1. Barbara Wentroble, *Prophetic Intercession* (Ventura, CA: Renew, 1999), p.87.
2. Ibid., p. 113.
3. Dutch Sheets, *Intercessory Prayer* (Ventura, CA: Regal Books, 1996), p. 220.

CHAPTER TWO

PRAYER IS
SHAKING THE WORLD

by C. Peter Wagner

In the first chapter, I talked about strategic intercession and how is it is growing as a prayer offensive and how it has been penetrating the territory of the enemy. However, I did not deal with the obvious question: Is this massive outpouring of prayer doing any good?

Is Our Prayer Doing Any Good?

This is a very important question for me, since I am intensely task-oriented. If I am working on a job I want to see that job done, or at least I want to be able to see considerable measurable progress toward the goal. I have been accused of being pragmatic by some of my critics, and all I can say in reply is that they are correct! If God has given me an assignment, I want to do whatever it takes to accomplish the purpose that He has in mind. I have always felt that obedience to God demands a pragmatic, results-oriented approach. If, for some reason, I don't get the job done, I find myself deeply disappointed.

Prayer over the long haul can get boring and discouraging if we do not see significant answers to our prayers. I know that there are some intercessors who have risen above that feeling, but I am not yet among them. If I pray, "Your kingdom come, Your will be done on earth as it is in heaven," I need to be encouraged by seeing tangible evidence of the hand of God at work. If our underlying purpose is evangelizing the lost, which it is, I want to see more people being saved and more churches being planted after strategic prayer than before we prayed.

Fortunately, our prayer action of the 1990s has been neither boring nor discouraging. I doubt whether any other decade in the history of the church could report such world-shaking answers to prayer. Answered prayer in the 1990s can fall into three interesting categories which I will describe. And then I want to conclude this chapter with some evidence of how earthquakes may relate to prayer and to show how prayer can be literally "*shaking* the world."

The Top Two Answers to Prayer

As I am able to develop a perspective on the history of the last ten years I would like to suggest that two answers to prayer stand out above the others. One primarily involves social conditions and the other involves evangelistic fruit. Both are important for the kingdom of God.

◆ **The dramatic end of apartheid.** South Africa was heading for a bloodbath. It had become obvious that the legal separation of blacks and whites called "apartheid" would have to come to an end sooner or later. Most scenarios for the end of apartheid included some form of bitterly contested civil war. But the prayer movement in South Africa, including dynamic pockets of strategic intercession, had arisen in a highly organized and coordinated form. The end of apartheid with no bloodshed was a social phenomena that no political scientist could have predicted. The battle, very obviously, had been won in the invisible world.

♦ **Church planting in the 10/40 Window.** At the beginning of the decade of the 1990s the AD2000 Movement had identified 1,739 significant unreached people groups in the 10/40 Window. The United Prayer Track and the Spiritual Warfare Network focused its efforts of strategic intercession on reaching those people groups. While it is true that the decade ended without all of those people groups moving from the unreached to the reached category, it is also true that by the end of the decade all of the groups but around 500 of them had been blessed with the arrival of an initial church planting movement. No other decade in history has seen this magnitude of missiological progress. I am encouraged!

Shaking Up the Four Major Anti-Christian Forces

In 1990 the four major anti-Christian forces on earth were Communism, Buddhism, Hinduism, and Islam. Literally millions of believers were praying that the grip that these ungodly forces had on peoples lives and destinies would be broken once and for all. High-intensity initiatives involving spiritual mapping, prayer journeys, prayer expeditions, published prayer guides, and strategic-level spiritual warfare specifically targeted one or the other of these obstacles to the gospel year after year.

What were the results?

◆ **Communism, to all intents and purposes, is gone!**
The grandiose Marxist experiment as a savior for society has
failed. Its theology of atheism never could and never will
capture people who are made in the image of God. Even nations which have retained Communism politically are no
longer able to stem the tide of the gospel. Communist China
is seeing the greatest harvest of souls in all of Christian history with an estimated 20,000 to 35,000 people being born
again every day. Professing atheist Fidel Castro, who ruthlessly persecuted Christians before the 1990s, found himself
sitting in a front-row seat in a crowd of 100,000 singing, dancing, banner-waving evangelicals in Havana's Revolution
Square before the end of the decade. Even in North Korea the
opposition to the gospel is not so much political and ideologi-
cal Communism as it is "Juche," an idolatrous worship of the
leader, Kim Jong-Il.

◆ **The spirits empowering Buddhism are now on the
run!** Buddhism no longer has the strength it once had in China
and both North and South Korea. Thailand used to be one of
the most resistant nations to the gospel, but dramatic changes
have taken place in this decade, and churches are now multiplying among Buddhists who are coming to Christ. Buddhism
has lost its grip on much of Southeast Asia. In 1998 the Dali
Lama called a high-level conference of Buddhist leaders in
Kyoto, Japan, with the main item on the agenda: What are we
going to do about all our Buddhists—especially our youth—
becoming Christians?

◆ **The spirits empowering Hinduism are badly battered!** In Nepal, the world's only Hindu kingdom, there were
only a few thousand believers at the beginning of the decade.
Jail sentences were the price that many of them had to pay for
following Jesus. However, by the end of the decade some

were estimating that there were 500,000 believers, and some considerably more. George Otis Jr.'s Sentinel Group has just removed Nepal from its strategic list of "Target Group 20" countries. North India was spiritually stagnant until the 1990s. Now the gospel is spreading with signs and wonders following all through the region. Some say the formerly resistant region of Sikkim is now more than 20 percent Christian.

♦ **The spirits empowering Islam are extremely nervous!** Islam was still the most formidable barrier to the gospel at the end of the 1990s. More than one billion people continue to be held in spiritual darkness by these principalities and powers. Prominent among them is the Queen of Heaven, frequently disguised as the Moon Goddess. But this fortress of darkness has developed widening cracks. For example, Indonesia is the largest Muslim country in the world. For years, however, the government has refused to publish their religious census because of their embarrassment over the unrestrained growth of Christianity. During the 1990s panicking Indonesian Muslims burned more than 1,000 Christian churches, but God used each one to advance, not to restrain, the spread of the gospel. Numbers of Muslim conversions are being reported in the Middle East as a result of visions, dreams, and miraculous healings where outward preaching of the gospel is forbidden.

These barriers to the gospel are not gone, but they are certainly much lower than they were before we launched the massive strategic intercession activities of the 1990s.

Widespread, Faith-Building Momentum

In this new millennium the gospel is spreading much more

rapidly than anyone could have imagined in 1990. We are in the midst of the greatest spiritual harvest that the world has ever known. Momentum is on the side of the kingdom of God at the present time in most parts of the world. There are two books, both written by friends who have been moving together with us through the 1990s, that are outstanding as field-based reports of this incredible spiritual momentum. You can search the missions sections of the largest Christian libraries, but you cannot find books like these written in past decades. I highly recommend these two books:

♦ *Beyond Imagination* by Dick Eastman. Eastman says that what I am calling spiritual momentum "is all part of a sweeping global revival and accelerating harvest of souls, marked by amazing signs and wonders, that I trust will inspire you to believe that the Great Commission may well be accomplished in our generation."[1]

♦ *The Move of the Holy Spirit in the 10/40 Window* by Luis Bush and Beverly Pegues. They say, "Around the world God is responding to the prayers of His children in supernatural ways. Doors are opening to the Gospel that seemed impossibly closed. God is using healings, miracles, dreams, visions, angelic encounters, and other divinely sent phenomena to bring not only individuals but entire families and even villages to faith in Jesus Christ."[2]

It would be impossible to summarize what these books tell us in just a couple of pages. But I want to make sure that we get some of the flavor of how prayers are being answered, so I will simply mention some randomly selected parts of the world with a few sentences of comment on each one, praying that this will be a great encouragement to those who have been praying fervently for more than ten years.

♦ **Africa.** Africa south of the Sahara is now more than 50 percent Christian. Some Muslims have become so insecure that they are trying to stop the spread of the gospel through genocide such as in Sudan. In early 1999 Reinhard Bonnke broke records with 500,000-person crowds in Benin. They thought it could never be matched, but later in the year crowds in Nigeria were even larger! More than 1 million persons made decisions for Christ in one campaign!

♦ **Latin America.** Revival fires have broken out in Brazil, Argentina, Guatemala, and other places. In Cali, Colombia, believers pack a soccer stadium holding more than 50,000 people for all-night prayer meetings four times a year. Guatemala's evangelical population has now reached 50 percent, and they probably have a higher percentage of born-again Christians than any other nation. The world's first transformed city, Almolonga, is also in Guatemala. It has around 90 percent born-again Christians and the last jail closed four years ago because there were no more criminals!

♦ **South Asia.** In Kashmir, North India, only 45 churches were planted by 1990 even though Christianity had been there since the time of the apostles. In the five years, 1990-1995, 50 new churches were planted. Then in only two years, 1995-1997, the next 50 churches were planted. This is the kind of momentum that the strategic intercession of the 1990s has produced.

♦ **North America.** We who live in North America may be too close to see it, but Christian people from other continents, sometimes whole planeloads of them, come here to learn about the power of the Holy Spirit. Revivals in Toronto and Brownsville are known around the world. We do not yet have the critical mass of believers needed to change society, but momentum is on the side of the kingdom of God.

♦ **Mexico.** One of the most notable results of Operation Queen's Palace recently occurred in Mexico where the Queen of Heaven's principal disguise is the Virgin of Guadalupe,

Mexico's "patron saint." Ana Méndez did strategic spiritual warfare at Guadalupe's annual festival in 1995 and that year it had the lowest attendance on record. She then led Operation Ice Castle which I mentioned in the last chapter. Subsequently she trained the "Lions" or the top intercessors for Operation Queen's Palace. In 1999 a believing priest, Guillermo Schulenburg, who was rector of the Basilica of Guadalupe for 33 years, blew the whistle on Guadalupe idolatry. He presented evidence to the Vatican that the supposed appearance of Guadalupe to Juan Diego in 1531 was a hoax. The upshot was that the Pope has now postponed the canonization of Juan Diego as a saint which had been scheduled for the year 2000. Ana Méndez says, "Hallelujah! We hit the Queen!"

♦ **The Jesus Film.** The Jesus Film, produced by Campus Crusade for Christ, is arguably the most effective evangelistic tool ever seen. Rivers of prayer have flowed through this incredible medium for presenting the gospel. At the beginning of the 1990s, 330 million had seen the Jesus Film, but by the end 2.9 billion had seen it, an increase of 2.6 billion! At the beginning of the decade there were 143 translations of the film, but by 1999 there were 547, an increase of 404 languages! And decisions for Christ? During the 1990s, 76.5 million individuals made decisions for Christ through seeing the Jesus Film!

Prayer and Earthquakes!

The climax of Operation Queen's Palace, "Celebration Ephesus," was a huge success. But the one most determining factor between success and failure was the massive Turkish earthquake of August 17, 1999. In the context of the Turkish earthquake, Chuck Pierce wrote, "Can praying actually create such a change in the spiritual atmosphere of a region that it affects the natural environment so dramatically?"[3] I think that the answer to that question is, "Yes!" Let's take a look.

Something Is Stirring in Turkey

Turkey is a very important nation for the global prayer movement. It is the hinge nation linking the 10/40 Window to the 40/70 Window. The average annual growth rate of Christianity in Turkey was 17 percent during the 1990s, but while the percentage is high, the hard numbers are minimal. Turkey had 261 believers in 1990, but only about 1,100 at the end of 1999. Turkey is a magnificent country with a population of 68 million, a strong foreign missionary presence, and official freedom of religion. Although 99 percent of Turks are Muslim, it is, for the most part, a quite nominal Islam.

Given those factors, Turkey should be 10 to 20 percent Christian by now, which would probably be a critical mass for the advance of the kingdom of God. However, a mere 1,100 believers will not do it. In July 1999, while I was praying for Turkey, I sensed that the Lord spoke to me and said that there will be 18 million believers in Turkey before Doris and I both die! For 200 years following the ministry of Paul and Timothy and John, Turkey was the center of world Christianity. I have very strong faith that the power of God will soon return to Turkey.

As I mentioned in the last chapter, it was in Ephesus, Turkey, that Doris and I received the divine assignment that became Operation Queen's Palace. We did what we could to call the International Spiritual Warfare Network and the global body of Christ to Turkey for the Celebration Ephesus event. Turkey originally was not a primary target for prayer, but only one of 64 nations of the 10/40 Window that we were concentrating on. However, it was the base for Celebration Ephesus and, because many intercessors would be traveling there, prayer for Turkey was greatly increased. In fact, the only book focusing on a single nation that we published during the whole decade was *Praying Through Turkey* by Andrew Jackson and George Otis, Jr. (Wagner Publications).

An Earthquake Can Change Things

The process leading up to Celebration Ephesus was not going well for us as far as support from the believers in Turkey was concerned. Strategic intercession was a new concept to many of the Turkish Christian leaders, and they were not altogether ready to endorse the activities of the Spiritual Warfare Network in their land. Many were praying, but I must admit that I was discouraged. Then, on August 17, 1999, the earthquake came! Everything changed! Because of the international news media, Turkey became a prime focus of prayer around the world, and it would remain so for the six weeks leading up to Celebration Ephesus on October 1.

Christians responded massively to this tragedy in a Muslim nation. The day after the earthquake, two relief teams from New Life Church of Colorado Springs arrived, instantly redeployed from Kosovo where they had been ministering. Within a week 25 to 30 workers had gone to Turkey from the World Prayer Center and New Life Church including two Eagles of God from Global Harvest Ministries. Teams of Christians arrived from Singapore, Hong Kong, South Africa, and other places. Astounded Turkish Muslims declared on national media, "We never knew that Christians loved us!"

Praying *for* Turkey!

At this point we changed the program of Celebration Ephesus. Instead of a praise and prayer event *in* Turkey, it became a praise and prayer event *for* Turkey. The top leaders of the churches in Turkey not only wholeheartedly attended Celebration Ephesus, but they ministered powerfully from the platform. No fewer than 500 believers, about half of the body of Christ in Turkey, were present. They were all deeply moved by the $75,000 offering for earthquake relief.

A Setback for the Queen

And the Queen of Heaven received a severe setback. The spiritual atmosphere over Turkey has changed. Police who had shut down places of worship have reopened them with a cheerful and friendly attitude. On December 26, 1999 the believers in Izmir were allowed to hold a city-wide Christmas celebration with 1,300 in attendance. All four local TV stations covered it, as well as two of the national TV networks. One woman said that, before Celebration Ephesus, no one in Turkey had heard of Protestants—they thought all Christians were Catholics. But the television featured *Protestants* praying for God's blessing on Turkey. The day after Celebration Ephesus several people said to that woman, "Are you one of those Protestants who love Turkey?" She was thrilled!

God's ways are mysterious, but I don't think that this earthquake could have been simply a seismographic phenomenon. The way I see it, the shaking happened in the natural world because of a previous shaking in the invisible world caused by fervent, strategic intercession. In fact Susan Ryan, one of the Eagles of God who went to Turkey right after the earthquake, recalled speaking with a Turkish Christian leader who had attended a conference back in 1997. The conversation was so important to her that she took notes. When she consulted her notes, she found that she had written, "[At the consultation in 1997] some prophets stated, 'An earthquake of historic proportions is coming to Turkey that would begin to unravel Islam and undo the social fabric of the nation!'"

Prayer Is Shaking the World

I believe that some day, when Turkey is blessed with 18 million believers, future historians will trace the origin of that movement to the earthquake of August 17, 1999. Yes, prayer is shaking the world!

Notes

1. Dick Eastman, *Beyond Imagination* (Grand Rapids, MI: Chosen Books, 1997), p.11.
2. Luis Bush and Beverly Pegues, *The Move of the Holy Spirit in the 10/40 Window* (Seattle, WA: YWAM Publishing, 1999), p. 49.
3. Chuck D. Pierce, "Prayer That Changes the Course of the World!" *Prayer Track News*, October-December 1999, p. 1.

CHAPTER THREE

MELTING THE ICE
OF THE 40/70 WINDOW

by C. Peter Wagner

Unlike the 10/40 Window, much of the 40/70 Window is covered with ice for several months of the year. But, whenever it becomes covered with ice, Springtime is coming! This capsulizes the hope of Operation Queen's Domain.

Why the 40/70 Window?

When I got back home from Celebration Ephesus, I was tired. Overseeing two years of the most intense strategic intercession on record was demanding, to say the least. I thought I deserved some rest and relaxation.

But not Chuck Pierce. No sooner did I unpack my bags than he said, "Peter, are you still the apostle of the global prayer movement?" I immediately recognized it as a rhetorical question and I waited for the other shoe to drop. It did! I had to admit to myself that even in Celebration Ephesus prayer leaders who were close to me and whom I respected very much had begun to drop me some very strong hints. "Without a vision, the people perish," they began to remind me.

But I had no idea where we were supposed to go from here. Chuck Pierce, however, put an end to my lethargy by saying, "Peter, as the apostle of the global prayer movement, you are the one responsible for casting the vision for all of us. If you do not seek the Lord for the next vision now, we are in danger of losing the momentum that God has given us for a whole decade!" So much for my desired R & R!

Inquiring of the Lord

I did what I knew that I had to do, and I began to inquire of the Lord. "Lord, where do you want us to go in the future?" This was no 40-day, or even 3-day, fast. As I recall, I spoke to God in the shower the next morning, and after breakfast the revelation began, thick and fast. Before noon, I was certain that He wanted us to concentrate on the 40/70 Window for the next five years. I knew that He wanted us to move from Operation Queen's Palace, which had ended in Celebration Ephesus, to Operation Queen's Domain. I knew that God wanted us to focus on that part of the world which contains, among other things, the largest number of non-Christians on the face of the earth, and that the principality of darkness most responsible for neutralizing the power of Christianity in that area was the Queen of Heaven. The surprising thing to me was that, previous to the day I received the revelation from God, I never had the slightest amount of interest in, or attraction to, the 40/70 Window.

So I shared these and a few other thoughts with my Global Harvest Ministries staff at lunch that same day. You would think I had lit a fireworks display! The immediate, high-voltage affirmation that this was truly what the Spirit is saying to the churches was incredible, in fact a bit overwhelming as far as I was concerned. From that moment, new information about the 40/70 Window started pouring in. Intercessor after intercessor began to feel fires of passion to pray for Europe, Eurasia, Russia, the Turkic Belt, Greece, Rome, Poland, Spain, Mongolia, North Korea, the Xinjiang Province of China, and numerous other places that rose up in their spirits. Soon after I announced the vision, I was told that three of my personal intercessors had already known that we were to shift to the 40/70 Window some time before I inquired of the Lord, but God did not allow them to tell me. I had to find out for myself.

The Challenge of the 40/70 Window

A whole cluster of considerations have helped the team at Global Harvest Ministries to understand why God might choose to focus our attention on the 40/70 Window. Many of the key intercessors in the global prayer movement have been responding by saying, "And don't forget . . ." or "Have you considered . . . or "The Lord has been saying the same thing to me" or words to that effect. Our knowledge of the 10/40 Window increased exponentially during the 1990s, and the same thing has begun to happen with the 40/70 Window.

One advantage that we have now, over what we had 10 years ago, is that the World Prayer Center is now well equipped with the technical infrastructure to serve as an unprecedented communications hub for researchers, intercessors, and prayer leaders. The Observatory unit at the World Prayer Center, under Derrick Trimble, is compiling an enormous spiritual mapping data base, and throughout Operation Queen's Domain they will be able to provide much of the strategic ongoing and up-to-date information that we need for informed strategic intercession much more rapidly than in the past. Our prayers will therefore be directed toward more specific targets than ever before.

Who Is the "Queen?"

Operation Queen's Palace concluded in Turkey, the recognized spawning grounds for worldwide goddess worship. As I have mentioned, we called it "Queen's" Palace because we consider the Queen of Heaven as a chief principality commissioned by Satan to keep unbelievers in spiritual darkness, and we have identified ancient Ephesus as one of her principal power centers where she formerly manifested in the person of Diana. We called it the "palace" because the temple of Diana (Artemis) in Ephesus syncretized, among other things, ancient Cybele worship, the Moon Goddess (Sin), and allegiance to Mammon (the temple was the first historical prototype of what we know today as the World Bank).

Not surprisingly, Ephesus was also the site chosen by the church of that day for the Council of Ephesus in 431 AD which helped legitimize the Mariolatry that is so widespread today by officially declaring that Mary is the "mother of God." Turkey and Ephesus are included in both the 10/40 Window and the 40/70 Window, and that is why we are looking at Turkey as our principal hinge nation. As we have seen, an incredible love for Turkey among believers worldwide was ignited by the earthquake and Celebration Ephesus.

A Counterfeit Mary
in the 40/70 Window

Mainly in the form of a Counterfeit Mary, the Queen of Heaven has deeply penetrated and corrupted much of the traditional Christianity of the 40/70 Window. I would imagine that statistics will soon show that those in the 40/70 Window whose primary spiritual allegiance is to the Counterfeit Mary will outnumber those whose primary spiritual allegiance is to Jesus Christ by many times over. As an unfortunate result, hard-core idolatry has become the norm *inside of* numerous Christian churches throughout much of the 40/70 Window and it presently constitutes an enormous barrier to lost people being saved. Latin America was in a similar situation up through the 1950s, but the spiritual climate there has changed radically.

Consequently, the 40/70 Window is the greatest area of dormant Christianity in today's world. This is why I have called this chapter, "Melting the Ice of the 40/70 Window." A spiritual ice age has engulfed this huge area of the globe. As I mentioned in the last chapter, revival reports have been emerging from many different areas of the world, including parts of the 10/40 Window. Believers are booking tours to fly to the revival sites and to see firsthand what the Holy Spirit is doing. Regrettably, very few Christian revival tours offer destinations in the 40/70 Window. The 40/70 Window contains more unsaved Christians than any other part of the world!

Many Are Burdened
for the 40/70 Window

In recent months, several key leaders of the International Spiritual Warfare Network (SWN) have been divinely drawn to the 40/70 Window. Even before Celebration Ephesus, I had asked Roger Mitchell of the United Kingdom (who has also written Chapter Seven) to undertake coordination of all of Europe's SWN instead of coordinating only Northern Europe as before. Roger has been one of the most dedicated and proactive of all the SWN regional coordinators, and his knowledge of the spiritual conditions of the 40/70 Window is second to none. Harold Caballeros, the equally effective coordinator of the SWN in Spanish-Speaking Latin America, has resigned that position in order to focus his energies on Spain, a key nation of the 40/70 Window. Cindy Jacobs has also prioritized Spain on her ministry agenda for the next ten years, and has written about it in Chapter Six. Speaking of Spain, it is notable that there is a lower percentage of born-again believers in Spain, traditionally a "Christian" nation, than in Japan, a notoriously resistant non-Christian country.

Gerda Leithgob of South Africa has been led to concentrate on Poland. She is convinced that Poland is the most idolatrous nation in the world. Ana Méndez of Mexico and Marty Cassady (author of Chapter Nine), have an unusual burden for Italy and Greece. Alice Smith has joined them in the focus on Italy. She feels that we should set up a base of 40/70 Window operations in Rome. Cindy Jacobs has recently received directive words from the Lord about ministry in Russia, including an urgent, time-sensitive assignment for Russian Jews (which she includes in her chapter). Martha Lucia of Christian International, another of our authors, had received prophetic instructions to target the 40/70 Window long before the rest of us.

Switzerland, considered by many the center of world finance, is in the 40/70 Window, and many prophetic intercessors are discerning a close relationship between the Queen of Heaven and the spirit of Mammon. I mentioned that the temple of Diana of the Ephesians was also the first prototype of our present World Bank. Chuck Pierce explains much of this prophetically in his chapter later in this book.

The 40/70 Window hosts Brussels, Belgium, the headquarters of the United Nations where the active promotion of the worship of Gaia, or Mother Earth, has become widely known. Some of her advocates feel that she, another clever disguise of the Queen of Heaven, should take her place as the recognized deity of the whole human race!

The Turkic Muslim Sector of the 40/70 Window

There are two major sectors of the 40/70 Window, one Christian and one Muslim. Let me quickly say that this should not cause us to neglect some of the other extremely crucial areas such as North Korea, Northern China, Mongolia, and Hokkaido Island of Japan. However, for the moment, let's look at the Muslim area.

The huge Muslim sector of the 40/70 Window is the heart of non-Arab, Turkic Islam, which draws considerable spiritual power from the Moon Goddess, another of the multiple manifestations of the Queen of Heaven. In a recent AD2000 report, Luis Bush has drawn our attention to the "Turkic Belt," also called the "35/45 Window," with nations clustered along the ancient Silk Road from Greece to China. Many of these nations are the former republics of the U.S.S.R. Intercessors in Singapore, which has one of the most advanced of all national prayer movements, sense that the Lord has been calling them for some time to focus on the Silk Road. Others will pick up similar intercessory burdens.

Signs of spiritual breakthrough in the Turkic Belt, which we include in the 40/70 Window, point toward a kairos moment, demanding fervent and concentrated prayer. For example, in 1990 there were only around 1,600 believers in the Turkic Belt, but by 1999 the number was over 43,000! It might well be that the breakthrough we have been praying for in the Arab Muslim world in the 10/40 Window will eventually come through a previous breakthrough among the Turkic Muslims, a bit further north in the 40/70 Window.

The Enormous Ripple Effect

As we concentrate our strategic intercession and our spiritual warfare initiatives on the 40/70 Window over the next few years, it will undoubtedly produce an enormous ripple effect. The ripples will rapidly spread out to the other nations and regions of the world which trace their cultural roots to peoples of the 40/70 Window. This means that nations like America, Canada, Australia, New Zealand, South Africa, Latin America, the Philippines, and other places will benefit immensely from Operation Queen's Domain.

It is more than likely that, as a result of intensifying our spiritual mapping research in the 40/70 Window, we will uncover some of the reasons why certain prayer initiatives in the countries and regions I have just mentioned turned out to have little effect. We have learned that in spiritual warfare on all levels, we are better off if we can get to the root of whatever form of demonic oppression we might be dealing with. Some roots of situations in South Africa, for example, might be found in Germany or some roots of situations in Peru might be found in Spain or some roots of situations in Australia might be found in England. I could go on and on. Operation Queen's Domain, therefore, promises to raise the level of strategic prayer not only in the 40/70 Window, but around the world as well.

Risky Side Effects

Whenever prescription drugs are advertised in America, the federal government requires that the possible side effects be made known to the public up front, even if those side effects are likely to occur only in very rare cases. I believe we need to be just as forthright in pointing out possible side effects of Operation Queen's Domain.

Experience in strategic-level spiritual warfare has shown that many times it is easier to deal with principalities of darkness over non-Christian religions such as Hinduism or Islam or Buddhism or animism or Shintoism than it is to deal with religious principalities who have found their way into Christianity itself. We faced relatively few of these as we prayed through the 10/40 Window in the 1990s. But, make no mistake about it, they will be among our chief foes as we tackle the 40/70 Window. They are especially strong when the religious spirits enter into unholy alliances with political spirits.

Such alliances erect barriers which we will constantly face in Operation Queen's Domain. We need to be aware of the predictable possibility of strong opposition from the entrenched leadership of the old religious wineskins of the 40/

70 Window, chiefly the Roman Catholic Church and branches of the Orthodox Church. They will likely be joined by some of the more liberal and ecumenical segments of traditional Protestantism and perhaps the Anglican Church.

While it is our duty to pray for these Christian churches, particularly that God will bring renewal and reformation and blessing to them, this is not the time for compromise or for seeking some least common denominator on which we might be able to agree. Tobiah and Sanballat might try to stall Operation Queen's Domain by beckoning us to sit down and talk, but my inclination is to respond with what Nehemiah said to them, "Why should the work cease while I leave it and go down to you?" (Neh. 6:3).

Time to Take a Stand

In my opinion, the time has now arrived to take a stand for truth and righteousness, particularly on the issue of idolatry, which in my opinion is the chief stronghold of the Queen of Heaven within Christian churches. God will not allow a dual allegiance. He is not pleased with those who attempt to worship the creature along with the creator (see Romans 1:25). Idols and pictures of dead individuals before whom people bow, worship, give gifts, offer praise, say prayers, genuflect, dedicate themselves and their relatives, light candles, burn incense, and expect to receive salvation have no place in Christian churches.

I have said several times that the underlying rationale for Operation Queen's Domain is the salvation of souls and the fulfillment of the Great Commission. If we continue to focus our minds and our hearts and our prayers on the ultimate destiny of multitudes of individuals, inside and outside of

Christian churches, who do not know Christ personally, we will maintain a perspective that will help us to overcome whatever opposition might be heading our way.

Melting Ice for a Fresh Start

Much of the 40/70 Window is exactly where Latin America was fifty years ago. Now we are seeing revival fires burning in much of Latin America, and the Queen of Heaven is losing her grip. We believe that, in a much shorter time, the spiritual ice covering the 40/70 window will be melted in the heat of revival fires burning brightly from Iceland to Siberia.

One thing that gives me hope is to realize that the 40/70 Window is a site of many of God's fresh starts: The Garden of Eden, Mt. Aarat, Ur of the Chaldees, Antioch, Wittenberg, Aldersgate, and others are all in the 40/70 Window. I believe that another fresh start is on the horizon for the 40/70 Window, and that we will actually see it happen in our generation as we obey God and join our global forces together in powerful prayer.

Yes! Springtime is coming!

CHAPTER FOUR

THE QUEEN'S FRIGID DOMAIN

by Chuck D. Pierce

Chuck D. Pierce is a widely recognized prophetic voice and leader in the worldwide prayer movement. He serves under C. Peter and Doris Wagner as Vice President of Global Harvest Ministries in relation with the World Prayer Center. He is also an ordained minister and serves as President of Glory of Zion International Ministries in Denton, Texas, which develops and covers the Eagles of God Apostolic Intercessory Teams that are sent on key prayer assignments worldwide. Chuck coordinates prayer for many of the major spiritual events and gatherings around the world, and also serves as Assistant Coordinator of the U.S. Spiritual Warfare Network along with Cindy and Mike Jacobs.

In the last chapter, "Melting the Ice of the 40/70 Window," Peter Wagner reminded us that the 40/70 Window is the greatest area of Christian dormancy in today's world. He says, "A spiritual ice age has engulfed this huge area of the globe. As I mentioned in the last chapter, revival reports have been emerging from many different areas of the world, including parts of the 10/40 Window. Believers are booking tours to fly to the revival sites and to see firsthand what the Holy Spirit is doing. Regrettably, very few Christian revival tours offer destinations in the 40/70 Window. The 40/70 Window contains more unsaved Christians than any other part of the world!" (p. 37).

"Always Winter, But Never Christmas"

Have you ever read C.S. Lewis's classic book, *The Lion, The Witch and the Wardrobe*? This has been a favorite tale of children and adults around the world. However, I am not sure we have seen the full spiritual implications of this allegory until now. In this story a young girl, Lucy, finds herself leaving her present world and entering another kingdom called Narnia. This kingdom was made up of many nations, but in this kingdom, it was "always winter, but never Christmas." What a terrible situation!

Why was this the case? It was because a White Witch, Jadius, the Queen of Narnia, had illegally gained rule and dominion of the entire region. She would then cast spells on any creature that tried to undermine her system of authority. Once the spell was cast, the creature or individual would become frozen and turn to stone. Therefore, the whole region was dominated by fear of the White Witch.

The White Witch also had the power of conversion. Lucy's brother Edmund was converted to her system once he followed Lucy into Narnia. The White Witch met him and deduced his weakness. She offered him false and temporary satisfaction in the form of a candy called Turkish Delight. This corrupted his nature and conscience. Therefore, a valuable player in the destiny of the nation was converted to fulfill her purposes and held by her dominion.

It is as if *The Lion, The Witch and The Wardrobe* is a parable of how the Queen of Heaven has taken dominion in the 40/70 Window and brought "winter, but never Christmas." As we consider this story in terms of the 40/70 Window, several questions come to mind. How does the Queen hold the resources of the area under her control? How does she keep the assets frozen so they cannot be used in the kingdom of God? How can we see the wealth and resources of this region transferred into God's covenant plan and availability? These are all questions that this and the next chapter should answer.

Understanding God's Plan of Territorial Authority

In both this story and in the 40/70 Window, the word *dominion* is a central theme. Dominion, therefore, is a good word to understand. Without understanding the word we can never take apostolic authority of a region. *Dominion* means the power to govern or rule, forcing a territory to recognize and subject itself to an authority or government. Even though dominion and authority can be greatly abused, there is an incredible principle throughout the Word of God concerning boundaries, dominion, and authority.

When the Lord placed Adam and Eve in the garden, He told them to "tend" or "watch after" the garden boundaries. They did not do well in this assignment. God continued to search for one through whom He could bless the earth, and He found a man named Abram. Abram lived in Ur, a Chaldean city whose predominant worship was of the Queen of Heaven. He was called out of this system of worship to follow a holy

God into boundaries of liberty and prosperity.

When Abram responded to God's call to leave the form of worship he was practicing and follow Him, the Lord formed an agreement, or made covenant, with Abram. His obedience to God released new authority and actually resulted in changing Abram's name to Abraham. This caused the nature of God to enter into Abram's life. We find in Genesis 15 that the Lord then established the boundaries of Abraham's inheritance.

Abraham's ongoing obedience would always move him just a little closer to occupying and receiving the full promise that God Almighty had spoken to him. Even though He did not see the complete fulfillment of God's word manifest in these covenant boundaries, his willingness to give up worship of the Queen of Heaven and follow God instead caused every family on the earth, including you and me, to be blessed (see Gen. 12:3). God's covenant with Abraham established a precedent for the human race that has been passed from generation to generation. God has an inheritance for us. Your inheritance is the portion God has agreed to give you on earth. Our inheritance or portion has boundaries determined with its allotment.

Jesus came to fulfill the redemptive plan of the Father on the earth. His obedience on the cross allowed us to be "grafted into" God's covenant plan. Being grafted into this plan has made us children of Abraham. This position gives us access to all the principles and promises that applied to Abraham's life. How does this apply to our portion or inheritance now on earth?

In the New Testament we find the same example of boundaries. In 2 Corinthians 10, Paul is discussing spiritual warfare. He then begins to declare the reality of his apostolic authority and the limit of its territorial boundaries. Verse 13 says, "We, however, will not boast beyond measure, but within the limits of the sphere which God appointed us—a sphere which especially includes you." I like what the New International Version says: "We will confine our boasting to the field God has assigned to us ..." Once boundaries are established we can unlock the inheritance that lies within these boundaries. Once we know our established boundaries, we have full territorial authority to move within those boundaries.

Apostolic Authority: Unlocking the Harvest Fields of the 40/70 Window

What a wonderful shift took place when the Lord impressed C. Peter Wagner to mobilize the army to enter the field of the 40/70 Window. This "shift of vision" created a key *kairos* time for the Body of Christ. *Kairos* means a set or opportune time for spiritual breakthrough. This word also means a key time to unlock what has been held behind closed doors or within illegal boundaries. In other words it is time to reclaim that which the enemy has taken illegal dominion of.

When the Lord began to shift our vision through Peter Wagner, we entered into the *kairos* time to unlock the field of the 40/70 Window. To do this unlocking, we must look at the Queen's illegal domination in this region. But we also must understand our apostolic sphere and authority. No illegal spiritual dominion will be able to stay in place if God's proper authority comes into place.

Within every *field* on earth, there is a harvest. When you study harvest in the Bible, you find that there was a short window of opportunity to gather the crops of the field. I believe we are entering into that window of opportunity and must begin to pray accordingly.

Each of us has a field of assignment. In that field are many resources. The most precious resource is people. When the Lord talks of harvest He expresses His heart for harvesting a field of souls on earth. In Matthew 9:36-38 we read, "But when He saw the multitudes, He was moved with compassion for them, because they were weary and scattered, like sheep having no shepherd. Then He said to His disciples, 'The harvest truly is plentiful, but the laborers are few. Therefore pray the Lord of the harvest to send out laborers into His harvest.'"

To operate in the Lord's call to harvest we must have eyes to see the multitudes, a heart of compassion, and a willingness to be sent to the fields to which the Lord has assigned us. To accomplish God's call to harvest there are material resources that have to be unlocked as well. Without the wealth necessary to harvest the field, it grows fallow. We will discuss this in detail the next chapter.

Notice how Matthew 9:36-38 introduces the commissioning of the disciples to go forth into the field. This is how apostolic authority begins. Remember these were the Lord's disciples. The word *disciple* means learner. However, the word *apostle* (or *apostolos*) means a special messenger, a delegate, one commissioned for a particular task or role, one who is sent forth with a message. Apostolic authority must be established in our field to unlock the harvest of that field. Therefore, we find in Matthew 10 the Lord promoting and commissioning His disciples into a new apostolic realm to go forth and cultivate the harvest where He sent them. This whole chapter is worth studying.

We find a great pattern in Matthew 10 for how the Lord cultivates and harvests a region. Let me summarize the chapter for us:

1. **He instructed His disciples concerning the scope of their mission**. He told them they were not called at this time to the Gentiles or the Samaritans, but rather that they were called to the Jews—the lost sheep of the house of Israel. We must understand the scope or boundaries of what we are called to. Within those boundaries we will have apostolic authority.

2. **He instructed them in the substance of their message**. They were to preach that the kingdom of Heaven was at hand. Therefore, in each territory you have to understand how God's Kingdom rule is to come to a territory with boundaries.

3. **He determined the works they were to perform**. They were to have power over unclean spirits and cast them out, they were to heal all kinds of sicknesses and diseases, they were to cleanse lepers, and they were to raise the dead. Everything the Lord had shown them by example and experience, they were to go forth and do in the fields to which they were sent.

4. **He also determined the amount of equipment or supplies they were to have in each field**. He wanted them to become dependent on the place they were going. This would be one of the ways that the Father would determine the unlocking of the region. If the people received them and gave to them and provided for their needs, then they would stay. If they would not receive them, they were to leave and not even take any dust from that territory. This would determine the Lord's judgment of the area.

5. **He explained what I call persevering, apostolic faith**. Disciples have to be willing to persevere even in the midst of persecution. There were false apostles and there were governmental controls that were against the kingdom of God. The Lord even explained that there would be family members that resisted this message in a territory. Therefore, without persevering faith they could never break open a territory.

So you see, apostolic authority is a real key to breaking open a territory. Apostles have the ability to forgive what has not aligned with the purpose of God in a territory. We find this principle in John 20. How apostles are received is a key measuring stick as to how the Lord releases blessings or judgments on a territory. Apostles also have authority over demons of a region. They have the ability to demonstrate supernatural power that draws a whole region to a life-giving God.

When we are approaching the area of the 40/70 Window we must think in terms of apostolic measures if we want to harvest those fields. This is what makes the 40/70 Window different from the 10/40 Window. There was very little apostolic authority in the 10/40 Window. We operated more in terms of a pioneering, birthing, penetrating work. But in the 40/70 Window we must call forth that which has already been birthed before but has never come into maturity. We must find the existing apostolic strength of each territory within this Window. We must assist those leaders, encourage their spiritual growth and maturity, and declare that their influence will begin to expand all over their area. Doing this will bring the harvest back into their region.

Ephesus: An Example of Apostolic Authority Unlocking a Region

I love the book of Ephesians. I love to study the revival in the city of Ephesus. We can find a record of this revival in Acts 19. Verse 2 contains the key question that changed the course of history as Paul arrived in Ephesus. He met Apollos, who was an apostolic figure in that region, and he asked him, "Did you receive the Holy Spirit when you believed?" Apollos had never heard of the Holy Spirit. He had only been baptized into "John's baptism." Therefore, Paul laid hands on him and they spoke with tongues and prophesied. He also baptized them in the name of the Lord Jesus. This started a chain of events that changed the course of Christian history and gave us a great example of apostolic authority affecting a region after the death and resurrection of the Lord Jesus Christ. We find a great pattern in the book of Ephesians. Paul prayed for the Ephesians to have spiritual insight concerning who Jesus Christ was. He then prayed that they would have insight into the hope of their calling in that region. He explained that they had an identity that was no longer of the world that is ruled by spiritual darkness. He gave explicit instructions on how they had been seated in heavenly places above all powers and principalities. He taught how the same Spirit that raised Jesus from the grave had also enlightened them and raised them into a position where they could have victory over their environment.

Paul admonished the Ephesians to understand a greater love and to be established in Christ's love. He then began to talk to them about their relationships. He actually said make sure all of your relationships are in God's order. Husbands and wives should have right relationships. Children and parents should have right relationships. Servants and masters should be right with each other in their daily relationships. Paul then instructed them to war against demonic forces that were gripping them and ruling their city. That's what Ephesians 6 is all about.

Paul knew there was a system of idolatry in Ephesus that was linked to Diana or Artemis. She was the ruling "strongman" and she had dominions and powers below her that infiltrated every aspect of society. These forces ruled their economic system, government system, education system, and worship system.

I love what Ephesians 2:1-3 says, "And you He made alive, who were dead in trespasses and sins, in which you once walked according to the course of this world, according to the prince of the power of the air, the spirit who now works in the sons of disobedience, among whom also we all once conducted ourselves in the lusts of our flesh, fulfilling the desires of the flesh and of the mind, and were by nature children of wrath, just as the others." And then Paul makes one of my favorite statements in the whole Bible. He boldly says: "**But God...**"

Paul knew that the love of God could change the course of society for the Ephesians. He knew the mercy and grace of God could create a new identity in this people and that identity could overthrow Diana's system that ruled their society.

The Queen's Illegal Hierarchical Domain

As I stated earlier, the Queen of Heaven, or Diana, illegally ruled this territory. And now God had commissioned His apostolic leadership to enter the territory and bring change. A hierarchical government can exercise authority in a region. If the government is unjust or dominant outside of God's sovereign power, its subjects become oppressed. The Queen has oppressed entire regions. How did the Queen of Heaven system overtake this and other territories?

There is a great article called, "The Origin of Sin and the Queen of Heaven."[1] This article reveals how the Queen of Heaven originated and adapted herself throughout both biblical and societal history. Most of us are fully aware of the practice of polytheism in early history. Most of these deistic beings were worshiped in idol form which was linked to either the moon or the sun.

Understanding the
Moon God/Goddess

It was believed that by communication with one of the "gods," one's mind could begin to experience "reality." Therefore, there was a great quest to discover the god behind all gods. By discovering what would be known as the god of wisdom, one's conscious mind and immortality could unfold. Therefore, the moon, when worshiped, would combine a cosmic reality with the mental aspect of man. Based on this belief, a whole system of worship around the moon and cosmic deities was formed.

The moon was considered the real husband of all women and was thought of as male. However, its cycles were linked with the bodily functions of women. In other words, the moon was considered the regulator and cause of menstruation. The moon was the source of the blood flow of human fertility and the empowerment of the mind. In pagan worship, it was believed that when women had their monthly cycle they were actually having sexual intercourse with the moon. There was also a belief that moonlight precipitated conception.

The widespread name of the moon god was Sin, the god of wisdom. As an offshoot of this, the moon god has a variety of other names which spans many cultures including Nanna of the Sumerians patron of Ur, Yerah of Ugarit, Kusuh of the Hurrians, Ilumquh of the Sabeans of Yemen, Soma of the Indo-Aryans, Yaho, Sofia and many others. The worship of these deities became astral and cross-cultural.

God determined to do something new on earth to break society out of this system. Therefore He communicated on earth with a man named Abram. As I mentioned before, God called Abram out of Ur of the Chaldeans. He was really leaving the worship of Nanna and Ningal. In Judeo-Christian tradition, Yahweh the true God was a God of revelation. From this time forward, He was known as a God that constantly was in communication with His people to show them how to live a prosperous, victorious life in His created earth.

However, as Roger Mitchell also points out in his chapter (see p. 101), the people on earth had grown accustomed to worshiping in this Moon/Sun system and were ruled by the gods that had been created in the system. These gods were idolatrous demon forces that would threaten the people if they tried to escape their power.

How did the Queen of Heaven threaten the people that worshiped her? She was known as a goddess of war. She had control over the agricultural system of the earth. Therefore their prosperity was linked with her blessing. The god of mammon would rule from the perspective of the Queen. She was also known as the goddess of fertility. We find this in the ancient Baal systems, which will be discussed in the next chapter.

Therefore the demonic forces linked with her would threaten a people with war, confusion, and chaos. The Queen would also threaten them with barrenness or poverty if they attempted to break free from her illegal system. So by using fear, this system ruled through the ages. This system was established in the city of Ephesus, a modern city of the early church world, and is still established throughout the world in many regions — especially the 40/70 Window.

Spiritual Global Warming in the 40/70 Window

BUT GOD! Paul knew that since he had been commissioned to go to the city of Ephesus by the Spirit of the Lord, he could have victory. When apostolic authority enters a territory a passion and authority of the Lord Jesus Christ is demonstrated. This fiery passion causes what was cold or even frozen to heat up and thaw out. Then the fire of God is loosed and the territory blazes with God's purposes.

It is important to understand Paul's strategy as he entered into Ephesus, as it is a good method for us to follow as we go forth in the 40/70 Window:

1. Paul found the existing apostolic leadership and released a new anointing in them. I've already explained how Paul did this with Apollos. Therefore the Holy Spirit began to manifest in the leadership of that region in a new way. The Bible even says he found twelve key leaders in the region (Acts 19:7).

2. Paul proclaimed the truth to the present religious system concerning the kingdom of God in an attempt to shift their paradigm into present truth. He reasoned daily for about three months in the synagogues trying to change their paradigm.

3. God worked unusual miracles through Paul's hands. Evil spirits left people's bodies, and many diseases were healed. Therefore, Paul demonstrated the authority of the name of the Jesus Christ above the name of Diana. Acts 19:20 says, "So the word of the Lord grew mightily and prevailed."

4. He confronted the Queen of Heaven in their economic system. A silversmith who made silver shrines of Diana called together all of the businesses that made these idols and said, "Men, you know we have our prosperity by this trade." He then explained to all of the businesses how Paul was causing their trade to fall into disrepute. If he continued to destroy Diana's magnificence, they would lose their means of supply.

5.   He brought the city structure ruled by a demon force into confrontation with the kingdom of God. Paul cast a demon out of a slave girl. This particular demon had territorial authority, and once it had been dispatched, it lost its territorial grip. This produced much confusion, but brought the city out of control of this demon force and released a major awakening of God in that territory.

This is what will have to happen in each geographical boundary of the 40/70 Window. Once the two patterns I have listed in this chapter begin to occur, that which has been frigid will have to thaw. The cold that has kept the seeds of the gospel that have been sown in this region from sprouting will have to submit to the fire of God.

To end with, many of you remember the story that we began with of the Queen of Narnia, the White Witch that illegally ruled Narnia. I love this story because once Aslan (who was a lion representing Jesus) began to move through the region all that the Queen had frozen was thawed and brought back to life.

Let's declare that the Lord Jesus Christ is now on the move through the power of His Holy Spirit and the 40/70 Window and the seeds of awakening will begin to spring forth as His fire ignites this region!

Notes
1. "The Origin of Sin and the Queen of Heaven" was posted in February 1999 on the website www.mat.auckland.ac.nz.

CHAPTER FIVE

HARVESTING THE WEALTH OUT OF THE QUEEN'S DOMAIN

by Chuck D. Pierce

A New Move of God in the Queen's Domain

Peter Wagner ended Chapter 3 by saying, "Much of the 40/70 Window is exactly where Latin America was fifty years ago. Now we are seeing revival fires burning in much of Latin America, and the Queen of Heaven is losing her grip. We believe that, in a much shorter time, the spiritual ice covering the 40/70 window will be melted in the heat of revival fires burning brightly from Iceland to Siberia" (p. 43).

He also stated, "As we concentrate our strategic intercession and our spiritual warfare initiatives on the 40/70 window over the next few years, it will undoubtedly produce an enormous ripple effect. The ripples will rapidly spread out to the other nations and regions of the world which trace their cultural roots to peoples of the 40/70 Window. This means that nations like the United States, Canada, Australia, New Zealand, South Africa, Latin America, the Philippines, and other places will benefit immensely from Operation Queen's Domain.

"As a result of intensifying our spiritual mapping research in the 40/70 Window, we will uncover some of the reasons why certain prayer initiatives in the countries and regions I have just mentioned turned out to have little effect" (p. 40).

I was privileged to lead a team of 40 intercessors, along with Cindy Jacobs and Bobbye Byerly, in Turkey as a part of Operation Queen's Palace to all seven original church sites that are listed in the book of Revelation. When we were at Pergamum, Cindy was leading the whole team in prayer and the Lord began to burden me concerning the issue of how the demonic structure that we described earlier in Chapter Four was holding the wealth of this entire region. When the demonic structure was released all over the world, the wealth of regions began to be used for works of darkness.

A Trip Around the World

The Lord then showed me a path that would take me to key cities around the world in order to to pray for a release and transference of wealth from the Queen of Heaven's cohort, Mammon. The Lord instructed me that if I would go and take a team to these places, I would see the wealth necessary for God's covenant plan for His future harvest on the earth released. Therefore, in February 2000, I led a team of intercessors around the world. The purpose of our trip was three-fold.

Firstly, we desired to connect with and cry out for apostolic leadership to rise up around the earth. I have already shared the importance of this in the last chapter. Our second objective was to test the communication system of intercessors that has developed over the last ten years. The key hub of this communication system is now housed in the World Prayer Center in Colorado Springs. We would communicate with these intercessors from anywhere in the world and instruct them on how to focus their prayers for spiritual breakthrough.

Our third, and key objective of the trip was that as we traveled from city to city, we would meet with key leaders and agree with them for a release of God's covenant wealth in each region. Strategic, prophetic intercessors pave the way for change with their prayers. We knew that if we broke down the spiritual forces that were holding back supply, wealth needed for the harvest ahead would be released. As we traveled, we came to one conclusion: *There is much revelation and much supply that the Body will need in days ahead to bring God's harvest plan for this season to completion.* In other words, we are going to need money and resources combined with revelation from God in order to complete the task He has given us.

That trip was the most focused intercessory journey I have ever been on. We would deal with the transference and understanding of wealth, and how to move forward in harvest. We visited the following cities: Chicago, Frankfurt, London, Berlin, Warsaw, Zurich, Singapore, Los Angeles, Denver, and Colorado Springs. In each city we would meet with leaders, pray, give gifts, and then go to key places within those cities to make declarations pertaining to God's will in releasing wealth for His Kingdom purposes. God moved so mightily that I do not have enough room in this one chapter to describe what went on in every city. But, I will recap a few items to give you an idea of how divinely directed we were in our travel.

Understanding God's Plan of Covenant Wealth

I love the following verse: "Every commandment which I command you today you must be careful to observe, that you may live and multiply, and go in and possess the land of which the LORD swore to your fathers. And you shall remember that the LORD your God led you all the way these forty years in the wilderness, to humble you and test you, to know what was in your heart, whether you would keep His commandments or not" (Deut. 8:1,2). This passage was the charge that the Lord gave His people when the time had come for them to go in and occupy the promise He had given 470 years prior to Abraham.

In every new season in church history, the Lord renews His vision, call, and purpose to His Body. We are just maturing in the season God has us in at this point in history. Therefore, He is saying the time has come for His people to enter into the promises He has released in their territories. These are promises that were never brought to completion by the previous generations. Every time we enter into a new season of history, the Lord does the following:

1. Releases new authority.
2. Commissions new leadership.
3. Causes a people to desire a new level of His holiness.
4. Communicates new strategies for victory.
5. Transfers the power to gain wealth so that His Kingdom purposes can be established.

Just as the Lord waited for 470 years before His people were ready to "enter in" and fulfill His promise He made to

Abraham, I believe He is waiting for us today.   Joshua was the leader that led God's covenant people into the covenant territorial boundaries declared in Genesis 15.   Joshua had to gain daily strategy over how to advance and "possess" God's inheritance that had been promised. He was God's leader for the season.

That is why having apostolic leadership, who understands the purposes of God and knows how to seek the Lord for revelatory strategy, is so important in every generation. In other words, if we are going up against our next obstacle, whether it is a city, a people or whatever, we must have individuals who can get instructions from the Lord on how to advance. We must have leaders who can lead us into our harvest fields. And we must know what to do with the spoils of war once we see them transferred into the Lord's Kingdom. What we learn from the examples in the book of Joshua becomes a lesson for us and produces principles of harvest that we should embrace today.

A Biblical Perspective on Wealth

First, we need to ask ourselves a very fundamental question: **What is the wealth?**

There are several ways to look at wealth in the Bible. However, the Lord tells us in Deuteronomy 8:18, "it is He who gives you *power* to get *wealth* that He may establish His covenant that He swore to your fathers" (emphasis mine). *Power* means vigor, strength, force, or capacity; whether physical, mental, or spiritual. *Wealth* means material substance, strength, and the spoils of war necessary to accomplish God's plan on earth.

The Bible has two basic attitudes toward wealth: one of

blessing from God and one in which wealth is worshiped as Mammon. Wealth is acknowledged to be a blessing from God. All the patriarchs became very wealthy. Solomon's wealth was seen as God's favor. Job had wealth, lost it, and then regained a double portion. Jesus also admonished us to multiply whatever we have (Luke 19). However, He did warn us that the pursuit of riches and pleasure could keep our faith from maturing. Jesus viewed money or wealth as a spiritual power (Matt. 6:24), therefore warning us not to let it become a rival with God.

A Proper Christian View of Wealth

The proper view that Christians should have toward wealth should only be for the advancement of God's Kingdom. With one of the greatest spiritual harvests ever witnessed by a generation on earth approaching, we need to begin seeing a transfer of wealth just as we read about in the book of Joshua. This is a season in history when wealth needs to be channeled into ministries that serve people and spread the gospel.

We must not fear the concept of wealth. We must not fear the concept of harvesting what God has given us to harvest. We must not fear multiplying and increasing. Money in itself is not bad. First Timothy 6:10 says that "love of money is the root of all kinds of evil." This does not mean that money is evil or amoral. The morality of money comes from the person using that money. One must never confuse money with the attitude of our heart.

We must also resist the idea that to be poor is spiritual. This teaching has its roots in pagan thinking termed docetism, which states that matter is bad and mind is good. Docetism has caused many problems in Christianity including the separation between sacred and secular.

We must also separate our personal worth from how much money we possess. Our worth is not linked with the money we have, but with our stewardship for God. Once these mindsets are overturned we are free to go forth looking at the harvest field that we are a part of and asking the Lord how we can harvest that field. This also gives us the vision and focus to overthrow anything that is set against the harvesting call that God has on our life for our field.

Avoiding the Traps

As we consider the issues of wealth, we need to be aware that there are very real traps we must avoid. When we go up against the enemy to fight for the transference of wealth into the kingdom of God, we must guard ourselves against the *love of money* (1 Timothy 6:10). *Philarguria* refers to avarice, which is the insatiable greed for riches, and covetousness, which is to inordinately or wrongly desire the possessions of others. If we are not careful, this is the fruit that money can produce in our hearts. Also, *deceitfulness of riches* (Mark 4:19) is another issue to be aware of. This deals primarily with the perceived power that comes with money. This produces an attitude of heart, which seeks to manipulate through false pretenses and appearances.

Money is good when it is a servant to us. However, when we become a slave to its dominion, we are in trouble. There were people in the Word who were cursed by wealth, or had impure motives to gain wealth such as Judas, Esau, Gehazi, Ananias and Sapphira, Lot, and Achan. They were trapped by impure desires.

As we move forward against the enemy, we must renounce

every issue of covertness that is tied to Mammon. We must detect any patterns in our own lives or in our family lines that are listed above. We must stay in God's covenant timing. When you get God's wealth out of God's time and way, you will get the curse that is on that wealth. Much money has curses attached to it. Therefore, if you don't know how to break the curse before you get the money, you will get the curse that comes with the money. This is what Malachi 3 is about. One way to break the curse off of money is to tithe and give offerings. We must pray for the Body of Christ in this area so that we come into an understanding of what it means to rob from God by withholding tithes and offerings.

Wisdom in Wealth

We must have a stewardship mentality before the Lord will release wealth. We must persevere against all odds and strategies of defeat. Perseverance is a necessary characteristic of God that is needed to establish the Kingdom. Proverbs 21:5 says, "The plans of the diligent lead to profit as surely as haste leads to poverty." Proverbs 17:16 says, "Of what use is money in the hand of a fool since he has no desire to get wisdom."

Again, money is an issue for us to understand right now. We do not have the mentality necessary to break open wealth in the Body. However, money is not the only issue we need to understand. Wisdom dismantles demonic structures. Therefore, if you are asking for money, ask for wisdom also. Third John 2 says there needs to be a balance between your soul and spirit to experience prosperity. This is a principle of covenant. There were judgments on those who did not steward what they were given in God's purpose and plan (Luke 19). This is the day of repentance, reconciliation, and multiplication.

Harvesting Canaan

This is a time when God is giving us strategy for the harvest fields that we are a part of. I showed in the last chapter how the enemy tries to freeze the supply of our fields. I used the White Witch from Narnia as an analogy to the Queen of Heaven today. I also discussed how apostolic authority could overthrow the powers and principalities that are holding back the supply necessary to advance God's Kingdom covenant purposes.

We find in Deuteronomy 8:18 that God spoke this to His people as He prepared them to get ready to go into the land He promised. He knew they would be in spiritual war with the god of Mammon. When you study Canaanite history, you find that the ruling god of the Canaanites was Mammon. The assignment or mission that Joshua and the tribes of Israel had to accomplish was transference of the wealth from all of the inhabitants of that region into God's covenant, Kingdom plan. Therefore, Mammon had to be defeated and the wealth held by its false worship transferred.

The Queen of Heaven and Canaan

How does this apply to the Queen of Heaven? It is because *the hierarchical structure of the Queen of Heaven rules over Mammon.* There are two economic systems on the earth. God has one economic system, and He teaches the necessity of us being stewards in this system. Satan has another economic system. Mammon rules this system. This god, through demonic forces, controls the administration, transfer, and distribution of the wealth within this system. Matthew 6:24 is a great verse to understand. It says, "No one can serve two masters; for either he will hate the one and love the other, or else he will be loyal to the one and despise the other. You cannot serve God and mammon."

Mammon controls all the world's finances, especially with regard to supply and distribution. Mammon is assisted by other demons in the administration, transfer, and relay of wealth. Mammon is both a prince of economics and prince of religions. As Marty Cassady points out in her chapter, Mammon is linked with the Babylon system. Proverbs 13:22 says that we can transfer the "chayil" of sinners to the righteous. Wealth or "chayil" means might, strength, power, army, forces, riches, spoils of war, fruits of warfare. In order to see that transfer take place, we must commit ourselves to strategic prayer for the transfer of wealth.

Results of Strategic Prayer for a Wealth Transfer

Here is an example of what can result from strategic prayer for a transfer of wealth. In the trip around the world that I described earlier, the issue of Jewish wealth stolen during the Holocaust came up and the Lord led the team in the following way: We first went to Berlin where the government that orchestrated those horrible years had existed. Next we went to Warsaw where much of the wealth was taken from the Jews. We were taken to a room where much of this actually occurred. We were then led to the place where the wealth was categorized. From there we flew on to Switzerland where much of the stolen wealth was stored. You can imagine the intercession this led us into. Immediate answers to prayer included the President of Germany asking forgiveness for the Holocaust only days after we prayed. The Lord has a path of life that breaks a structure of death and control.

An Associated Press article dated February 16, 2000 stated, "Germany's president delivered an emotional address to Israel's parliament Feb. 16, asking for forgiveness for the Holocaust. Johannes Rau, an Evangelical Christian, spoke to the Knesset in German, a historic first, saying he bowed his head before the 6 million victims, news reports said. Legislators applauded respectfully, but some stayed away in protest, saying they did not want to hear German spoken in parliament. A legislator who had watched Nazi troops round up Jews in the Warsaw ghetto called German 'the language of Satan.' ...Rau, a longtime friend of Israel, also toured the Yad Vashem Holocaust Memorial. He wrote in the guest book, quoting German clergyman and Nazi dissident Dietrich Bonnhoeffer, 'Perhaps Judgment Day will be tomorrow. In that case, we would happily stop [working] for a better future, but not before.'"[1]

Since our return we continue to see tangible answers to our prayers. The February 28, 2000 issue of *Time Magazine* carried an advertisement stating, "Suppose Your Family Had a Holocaust Era Insurance Policy and You Just Didn't Know About It?" The ad provides information in 23 languages on the claim resolution process.

Then on February 29, 2000, an Associated Press report revealed that British museum directors published a list of 350 art treasures in their galleries that they believe may have been stolen by the Nazis during World War II. This first-of-its-kind report lists works worth tens of millions of dollars that may stem from Nazi looting of hundreds of thousands of paintings and sculptures that once belonged to Jews and other victims of Hitler's Germany.

Strategic Prayer Can
Also Result in a Government Shift

The Lord also led us to pray over the residual issues of Nazism as we were praying over the Holocaust. Another immediate and dramatic answer to the team's prayer came on February 29, 2000 when Jorge Haider, leader of Austria's Freedom Party, resigned amidst criticism from the international community including the European Union and the United States. Past statements by Haider have expressed admiration for Adolf Hitler's employment policies, and described World War II concentration camps as "punishment camps." His resignation will help neutralize the divisiveness and violence that erupted after his election, and cause many to question the resurgence of pro-Nazi ideologies.

These are just a few examples of what happens when we begin to release focused, strategic, intercessory prayers and join with those who have been praying through the decades. The enemy must release the wealth of this region back into God's covenant plan. If we pray, we will see miracles.

Issues of Wealth in the
40/70 Window

The following is a list of some of the issues that the enemy uses to control wealth in the 40/70 Window that we should be aware of as we pray for the transference of wealth into the Kingdom of God:

Trade routes (e.g. Silk Road)

Stretching 4,030 miles from Istanbul, Turkey to Beijing, China, the Silk Road stands out as one of the most renowned and prosperous land trade routes in history. The 700th anniversary of Marco Polo's incredible 24-year journey was celebrated in 1995. Large portions of the 19-country expanse of the Road have been opened to international tourist trade. Besides being a route for bartering silk, jewels, and gold the Silk Road was also a critical path for exchanging cultural, philosophical, and religious ideas. Pakistan, Afghanistan, Tajikistan, several of the countries along the Silk Road, now use this ancient path to sell opium. Afghanistan is the world's largest producer and exporter of opium.

Prayer Point: Karl Marx, the father of twentieth-century communism, said, "Religion is the sign of the oppressed creature, the heart of a heartless world, and the soul of soulless conditions. It is the opium of the people." Ask God to remove the spiritual opiate of religion that dulls those under the rule of communism (and former communist states) from coming to the Risen and Living Christ.

Nautical supremacy (England, Spain, France, Rome, Norsemen/Vikings)

For many countries of Europe, the power to expand a nation's property holdings or increase wealth was reflected in their nautical strength. England gained the notoriety of having the "sun never set on the British flag," mainly as a direct result of their command of the world's oceans. Spain plundered the wealth of the Americas, filling their ships with gold that was paid for with the blood of entire cultures, such as the Incas. The Norsemen opened a migratory path to North America. One person who exemplifies the importance of modern day nautical superiority was the Greek shipping tycoon, Aristotle Onassis. (By the way he was born in Smyrna and left the country under the attack of

Ataturk's army.)

Prayer Point: "The end of a thing is better than its beginning; The patient in spirit is better than the proud in spirit" (Ecc. 7:8). In the beginning, "the Spirit of God was hovering over the face of the waters." In the end, it is the tradesmen of the sea who will mourn the fall of the Babylon system (Rev. 18:19). Now at the close of the ages, ask the Spirit of God to hover or brood over the issues of seafaring trade and nautical superiority to redeem a "better than" end.

European Union

While there are many topics that are hot for European Union members to address, perhaps none is as debated as the Eurodollar. One of the theories entertained by some economists is that by bringing Germany into a common European currency, it will stave off or eliminate the possibility that Germany will wage war on their neighbors again. Others see the Eurodollar as an opportunity to consolidate in order to gain an upper hand on the U.S. dollar. Still another group sees the common currency plan as having a disintegrating effect on national sovereignty.

Prayer Point: In the Gospel of Luke, Christ says, "For nothing is secret that will not be revealed, nor anything hidden that will not be known and come to light. Therefore take heed how you hear. For whoever has, to him more will be given; and whoever does not have, even what he seems to have will be taken from him" (Luke 8:17-18). Despite the efforts of some political and economic analysts to speculate on the future of Europe, truly only God knows the "end of the matter." Pray that the Lord will reveal the hidden things, that the church in Europe will hear, and that a transfer of wealth will be accomplished according to God's plan and order.

Swiss Banks

Recent big news in the media has been the revelation that during World War II the Nazis hid millions in gold stolen from Jews in Swiss banks ($300 million to be exact, which has an estimated worth of $2.6 billion today). The irony is that the gold, as well as other assets seized, became the financial leverage for Hitler to purchase raw materials for waging war. U.S. Undersecretary of Commerce Stuart Eizestat's recently released report revealed that 41 nations have current gold holdings pillaged during World War II, which have an estimated value of $5.6 billion. A thorough search of some 15 million documents also exposed that the United States and Britain have pillaged gold. A question recently surfaced regarding the Vatican's role concerning Nazi gold.

Prayer Point: While neutrality has the appearance of being a benign approach to conflict resolution, neutrality in today's political arena is a façade. The two main issues for prayer are for the Swiss to take an intentional step toward submitting to the leadership of Christ, and that faith will rise for the wealthy of the world. "It is easier for a camel to go through the eye of a needle than for a rich man to enter the kingdom of God…but not with God, for with God all things are possible" (Mark 10:25, 27b).

German Industrialization
(Includes the Marshall Plan)

The industrial nature of the German worker helped create the pre-World War II industrial strength that gave Hitler the ability to wage his war. After the war, allied forces devastated Germany and Japan. The European Recovery Program, commonly called the Marshall Plan after U.S. Secretary of State George Catlett Marshall, was the United States' answer to assist these nations in recovery. The U.S. put up $13 billion dollars in aid. The amount was considered a small sacrifice to stave off Soviet pressure to move European countries over to a communistic style of government.

Great Britain and France called other Europeans, including the Soviets, together in Paris. When Soviet delegates learned that the U.S. insisted on their cooperation with the capitalist societies of Western Europe and an open accounting of how funds were used, they left Paris and established their own plan to integrate Communist states in Eastern Europe. An economic curtain divided the continent. This singular event divided the continent, but the Marshall Plan funds used to rebuild the country are largely responsible for the success of today's German industry (auto, technology, communications, and banking).

Prayer Point: There is a principle that is built into the blessing of others. Ask the Lord to bring about an awareness and appreciation for what has been sowed into post-World War II Germany. "To whom much is given, from him much will be required" (Luke 12:48). German engineering and ingenuity are world-renowned. Therefore, ask also that creative flow and financial blessing will be reaped in the kingdom of God.

The Vatican

The property holdings of the Roman Catholic Church are second to none. There is also considerable speculation that the Vatican has a large amount of wealth deposited in Swiss banks. There seems to be a very distinct attachment between the Vatican and Switzerland. The evidence that the armed guards for the Vatican are "Swiss Guards" says that there is more than just a religious deference. We continue to try to uncover how much and where the Vatican keeps its wealth.

Prayer Point: The Vatican is located in an area of Rome

known as the Holy See. There is a lot of mystery surrounding the Roman Catholic Church and its government agencies in the Vatican. Ask the Holy One of Israel to remove the veil that we may look into and "see" how God wants to unlock the Vatican and those under the cloak of religion.

Organized Crime

When governments become oppressive in their stance towards free-market trade and begin to either impose strict government control or interfere with supply-and-demand commodities, a group will organize to provide the goods that society is lacking. In most cases these provisions will be through the underground or illegal avenues. Organized crime syndicates operate in nearly every country of the world. However, there is nowhere in the world where they are more organized and yield such a vast amount of control than in the 40/70 Window.

Most of the countries where organized crime has found fertile soil to germinate are Russia and the former Soviet Union satellite states (i.e. Hungary, Ukraine, Tajikistan, Uzbekistan, Kyrgyzstan). Leaders in many of these nations have agreed that the greatest criminal danger to the region results from narcotics-related crimes. Poland is one of Central Europe's largest narcotics exporters. It is also the main transfer route for cars stolen in Western Europe, which end up in countries east of Poland. Other countries have their own problems. Organized crime costs Hungary roughly $500 million a year, according to Hungarian police.

Prayer Point: Social infrastructures built under the oppression and dominance of criminal activity are vulnerable to losing essential moral elements of their cultural identity. Survival of the fittest becomes the law of the land. However, the Lord is the advocate for the fatherless, the widowed, and the oppressed. Ask the Lord to carefully dismantle the systems that create bondage to oppressive social structures. Call out for the church to rise up into the place of serving communities where organized crime has become the norm for daily living.

Feudal Systems (Monarchy and "Old Money")

Besides the Vatican, the royal families of Europe have maintained the strongest hold on "old money." Under the monarchial and feudal systems of the Old World, kings, queens, emperors, dukes, barons, and every level of lord gained wealth at the expense of vassals under their "protectorate." Much of the property, deeds of claim, and wealth have been passed on from generation to generation. While there has been a shift away from royalty, there remain those who have made their money under the watchful and supportive glance of royalty. The connection between the church (namely the Catholic Church) and the thrones of Europe are unmistakable.

Prayer Point: There are several condemning references to the "kings of the earth" in the book of Revelation. In spite of the inclination for these "kings" to be at enmity with the Almighty, Christ remains as Ruler (see Rev.1:5). Ask God to send a fresh word through the Holy Spirit to "convict the world of sin, and of righteousness, and of judgment" (John 16:8). Pray that some of these "kings" will be rescued, albeit by fire.

Launch Out for a Transfer!

I believe the word for us at this time is: *Launch out!*

The word *launch* means to hurl, discharge, or send off; to

send forth with force; to set in operation; to start on a new course, career or enterprise; to throw oneself (into) with vigor. Fishermen would take a circular net with weights and cast it out on the water. It would then sink into the water, a drawstring would be pulled, and the catch brought in.

In Luke 5, Peter had been doing this all night and had brought in nothing. Therefore he was exhausted, frustrated, and really did not know what the next move should be. Jesus then gave him direction that was contrary to his thinking. He said, "Launch out and go deeper!"

Peter displayed his doubt that Jesus really could understand his daily situation and the method of gaining the supply he needed. However, when he obeyed Jesus' word, he brought in an overwhelming catch that was not only enough for him, but met his partners' needs as well. *The miracle overcame the doubt.* Then the Lord said, "now go forth and catch souls (mankind)." After this demonstration, the disciples went forth evangelizing.

As we begin to pray for the 40/70 Window, the Lord wants to do the miraculous in our everyday lives. This will cause supply to be released that will meet our needs. But the real issue is that this will cause faith to be released that will propel us forward to achieve God's Kingdom purposes in this particular territory. As we see Him move in our lives then we can have faith that this entire region can be freed from the clutch of the Queen of Heaven and Mammon.

Strategic prophetic intercession must be properly aligned with apostolic government for spiritual breakthrough and harvest to occur. Therefore, we must continue to pray that the communication system between intercessors becomes very effective and that it connects properly with apostolic leadership and vision. This communication is a vital key as we focus on our mission field of the 40/70 Window. Both intercessors and apostolic leadership will have to blend for us to become successful.

So get ready to be launched into a new dimension as we pray for the release of harvest that has been held up by the enemy in the 40/70 Window!

Notes

1. Karin Laub, "A First: German President Addresses Israeli Parliament in German, 02-16-2000," copyright 2000 Associated Press: The Archive website.

CHAPTER SIX

FIRE AND ICE:
FOCUS ON RUSSIA AND SPAIN

by Cindy Jacobs

Cindy Jacobs is an ordained minister who has often been called a "spiritual warfare specialist." She travels to many nations meeting with leaders and intercessors with a heart to tear down satanic strongholds over their cities, states, and nations. Cindy is president and co-founder (along with her husband, Mike) of Generals of Intercession which is a missionary organization devoted to training in the area of prayer and spiritual warfare. Cindy also serves as the coordinator for the U.S. Spiritual Warfare Network, a network of ministry leaders who strategize for the United States on the spiritual warfare prayer level, seeking national revival.

As God is focusing the worldwide prayer movement on the 40/70 window, it is critical that we understand the needs and spiritual significance of two strategic nations, Russia and Spain. I call this chapter "Fire and Ice" because both of these countries have these two extremes in the hearts of the people. There is tremendous passion to see the icy heart of the nation burn fervently for Jesus Christ. My interest for both of these nations is of a prophetic nature. I see them as keys to reaching the world for Jesus Christ.

RUSSIA

A Prophetic Dream

The call to encourage prayer in Russia came to me during a dream. The dream was really what I would call a night vision or prophetic dream. I saw a scene of a church that had been bombed. The domes were destroyed. Across the way from the church was what looked like an abandoned airfield. A feeling of intense grief came over me as I awakened from the dream. The Lord then spoke to me and said, "I'm calling you back to Russia."

I then phoned a friend of mine, Bill Greig, Jr., who has a deep love for Russia and relayed the dream to him. He knew exactly what it meant. The church was one located outside of St. Petersburg which had been bombed by the Nazis during World War II. The field I envisioned across the way was the burial ground for the 90,000 Nazi soldiers who were killed in the siege of the city, which was at that time called Leningrad. Staggeringly, an estimated 1.5 million Russians (mostly civilian) died during that time as well.

The Deciding Factor

The dream and my conversation with Bill Greig, Jr. piqued my interest in Russia and I started researching what ongoing intercession was occurring for the nation. I found that for the most part, people prayed and went to Russia immediately after the fall of Communism, but interest has waned quite a bit since that time. In the meantime, the nation is in dire straights. Crime, gangs, and the Russian Mafia are huge, terrifying threats. The nation is desperately in need of prayer.

In talking to Bill Greig he gave me a profound insight into this serious deterioration. He said, "Cindy, I was praying one day for Russia and asking the Lord how the nation has gotten into this terrible condition and the Lord told me, 'No prayer.'" His comment intrigued me as he went on to explain that for years we prayed for China and the suffering church there. However, because the Soviet Union had been perceived as our enemy during the Cold War years very few have prayed for Russia with the same urgency.

As Bill told me this, I had a flashback to my days in kindergarten when I spent time under my desk during air raid drills. We were preparing for imminent attack from the Soviets. Many were so affected by the fear brought on by the Cold War that they built bomb shelters in their backyards. The effect of this threat upon the United States' culture still remains. So we prayed for China and have seen a great revival. But, we have neglected today's Russia.

It is my prayer that God will open your heart to Russia, at times the forgotten nation, and pray. Russia is a nation at the crossroads. It could either revert back into the strangleholds of yesterday or emerge as a giant that sends missionaries across the world. Our prayers will be the deciding factor.

In addition, as I explain later, the lives of many Russian Jews also depend on the prayers of God's people.

The Russian Need

Russia's unique geographic location, astride both Europe and Asia, has influenced its history and shaped its destiny. It is the world's largest country, spanning eleven time zones. One 1998 estimate puts the population at approximately 146,120,000. According to some information I received, there are 650,000 orphanages, and 1,000,000 children living on the streets in Russia. Only .7% of the population in Russia is Protestant. Some statistics show that there are only 473 missionaries working in this huge nation. There are 101 indigenous languages spoken in the federation. Many of the people, such as the Ural Turkics, still need Bible translations in their languages.[1]

The Introduction of Christianity

The history of Russia is so long and complex that it is impossible to do it justice in this short chapter. I hope to give you intercessors, for whom this book is written, a desire for more study so you can pray effectively. Rather than simply give you statistical facts, I want to share what I have found to be root problems that need to plucked up through spiritual warfare in order to free this giant Russian Federation.

The earliest written Russian history, *The Primary Chronicles*, states that the name Russia comes from a tribe of Vikings called the Varangian Russes. The first state, Kievan Rus (modern day Kiev) was an important trading center. Kiev, although now in the Ukraine and not in Russia itself, is also important to this chapter because it is the entry point of Christianity for Russia.

Prince Vladimar made Christianity the state religion around

988 and instituted the first state church. As a result, the East Slavs, who had been largely nature worshipers, largely became Christians. The Russian Orthodox have churches in almost every city today, even the Muslim ones. If these churches were to experience revival and break away from moral and other forms of corruption, they could simply use the existing buildings for the glory of God.

A Bloody Past

One main thread that runs through the history of Russia is the existence of massive amounts of bloodshed. One of their rulers, Ivan the Terrible, the first to be called a czar, killed church leaders and even murdered his own son in a fit of anger. While we were in Moscow several years ago, we learned that Ivan the Terrible put out the eyes of the architect of St. Basil's Cathedral in Red Square so that he could never build a more beautiful building.

Cities such as St. Petersburg were built upon the bodies of dead peasants who are literally part of the foundation of the city. These slain souls were never given funerals. Their bodies were just covered up. Red Square has that name for a good reason.

Many of you know of the Russian premier, Joseph Stalin. During his time in power, he closed 55,000 parishes, but left 100 open to show that there was "religious freedom" in the country. In addition, he executed 50,000 Orthodox priests. Surely this blood cries out from the ground.

I mentioned the bloodshed during World War II earlier. Derrick Trimble of the Observatory in the World Prayer Center in Colorado Springs found a map dotted with gulags (forced labor camps) and concentration camps from this time period.

The Nazis built concentration camps and put the Jews in them as they advanced into Russia, often with the help of the locals who welcomed the Nazis. Of course, many Christians were killed during this time as well.

As I have been praying for Russia it is clear that the land is defiled from this bloodshed and thus is under a curse (see Lev. 18:25, Hosea 4:1-3). The many murders, wars, corruptions, Communism, and pogroms against the Jews have all stained the ground with sin. (For more understanding on the subject of healing the land see Alistair Petrie's, *Releasing Heaven On Earth,* Chosen Books, available after September, 2001.)

Rasputin's Curse

The occult has also been part of the cursing of the land as practiced through men such as Grigory Yefimovich Rasputin (1872-1916) who were devastatingly evil. Rasputin believed in the doctrine that one was nearest to God when feeling "holy passionlessness." He felt that the best way to reach this state was through sexual exhaustion that came after prolonged debauchery.

Rasputin was first called to the palace by Nicholas and Alexandria in 1908 to stop the bleeding of their hemophiliac son. During this time the court was delving into mysticism and the occult. Desperate for help for their son, Nicholas and Alexandria became greatly deceived and believed Rasputin's warning that the destiny of both the child and dynasty were irrevocably linked to him. Could this divination have brought a curse upon the land? I believe so. Rasputin became increasingly licentious; preaching that physical contact with him had a purifying and healing effect.

In an effort to kill him, Rasputin was poisoned by three nobles. The poison didn't kill him, so they shot him. Somehow, he still survived. Finally they bound him and threw him in the Neva River. His death was most likely by drowning.

Why did I spend so much time in this chapter on this man? It is because we have seen the effect that a man like Rasputin can have on countries. For instance, in Argentina, José López Rega, the social welfare minister who served under Juan Perón in the early 1970s, openly cursed the nation when he lost power in 1976. The once flourishing Argentine economy dramatically declined in the years that followed. In 1990, Doris Wagner and I traveled to Argentina several times and, with the help of many key Argentine leaders and intercessors, we were able to break the curse through strategic level warfare. Since that time dramatic changes in the economy and spiritual climate of Argentina have occurred, and the nation continues in revival. Could the same thing happen in Russia?

The Plight of the Russian Jews

I have intentionally left the issue of the Russian Jews for last in this section on Russia because there is a special urgency for prayer that must be highlighted.

In a recent meeting of the Apostolic Council of Prophetic Elders (ACPE), God clearly spoke to us that there was great danger of pogroms arising which would be a great danger to the Russian Jews. While we felt there is a short time frame in which persecution could arise, we are aware that prayer changes history and so this prophetic word is a call for intercession on their behalf.

In order to understand more about this situation, you must understand pogroms. A pogrom is a frightening Russian word which means devastation, riots, or mob attack. The dictionary definition is an organized massacre especially of Jews. The first extensive pogroms followed the assassination of Tsar Alexander II in 1881. While only one Jew was associated with the assassination, false rumors incited mobs in more than 200 cities. Pogroms were common from 1903 to 1946.[2]

When the prophets at the ACPE meeting received the word of the Lord concerning the Russian Jews, most of us did not know anything in the natural that was going on inside Russia in this regard. However, since that time we have been receiving sobering reports. A recently restored synagogue was vandalized in 1999 by an anti-Jewish group boasting chapters in at least 10 cities. Reports have been made to the U.S. Senate Foreign Relations subcommittee that anti-Semitism is on the rise in Russia.

An estimated 500,000 Jews remained in Russia as of March, 1999. The immigration of Russian Jews has increased 100 percent in early 1999. There are now approximately 3,000 Jews per month immigrating. At this rate it would take 12 or more years for them to all immigrate. A recent article in the Hebrew press read: "It is one minute before pogroms,"[3] meaning that at any minute a riot against the Jews could begin.

This is a sobering call to prayer. What if the Jews had left Germany before Hitler began to annihilate them? We must cry out to God for Russia and pray for protection for the Russian Jews.

In Summary

I cannot close this section without saying the Russian people are incredibly creative. They are famous for their artisans and very well could be the modern day Bezaleel whom God anointed with exquisite workmanship skills for the temple in the wilderness (Exodus 31:2).

There are many wonderful reports out of Russia. Gospel Light Publications has produced Sunday School material which presents the gospel in such a way that Russian leaders in the Orthodox Church want to get it into all of their churches. Remember, they're the ones with all those wonderful buildings to fill as revival comes and sweeps away that which doesn't please the Lord, and Russia becomes filled with His Glory.

SPAIN

A few years ago, my good friend Harold Caballeros asked me if I would be interested in going to Spain to teach. I had received invitations from Spain in the past but felt this was the time to go. Another special reason that I wanted to work in Spain was because of my son-in-law, Tom, who was born in Cadiz, Spain.

The first year that I went to Spain (1998), I knew God had a special call for me in that nation. Two of my friends, Paco Garcia and Harold Caballeros, have a special vision to plant one thousand churches in Spain and Portugal. In order to understand the vast need, it is important to know some very sad statistics.

Spain has a population of 40,460,055. Out of these millions of Spaniards, there are only 88,547 believers. That's only .02 percent of the population. Furthermore, there are 7,400 "poblaciones," which are settlements, towns and cities that do not have an evangelical church.

The nation of Spain is known for its beautiful cities. It is one of the largest countries in Europe and occupies five-sixths of the Iberian Peninsula. Portugal makes up the other sixth. The Lord gave me a prophetic word on my first trip that these two nations together would display the redemptive gift of intimacy with God.

Spain is strategic for all of Europe and for Africa as well because Africa is only eight miles south of Spain across the Strait of Gibraltar. I believe that when the Spirit of God moves in Spain, He will use this nation to evangelize Europe as well as northern Africa where so many unreached people groups live.

The Spanish Inquisition

As we pray for Spain, there are two historical facts to bear in mind. They are the Spanish inquisition, and the slave trade.

Inquisition is derived from a Latin verb *inquiro* (inquire into), which emphasizes the fact that the inquisitors did not wait for complaints to come in, but rather sought out heretics and other perceived offenders. The procedure called for giving the suspect time to confess before bringing him or her before the inquisitor. Torture was then used to obtain confessions and information about other heretics.

The Catholic monarchs, Ferdinand and Isabella, requested a special inquisition from the Pope to combat apostate former Jews and Muslims as well as heretics. The first inquisition operated in Seville where the inquisitor, Tomas de Torquemada, started a propaganda campaign against the Jews. In 1492 he persuaded Ferdinand and Isabella to expel all Jews who refused to be baptized, which amounted to about 170,000 of the monarchs' subjects.

This expulsion is interesting in the light of the fact that the Jews had faithfully served the monarchs of Spain, providing the educated elite. But, jealousy erupted against them because of their wealth. There is no doubt that those in power must have gained a great deal of fortune through the confiscated properties of the Jews. During this time some Jews went underground by professing to be Christians, but were later denounced as being secret heretics.

By one count, at least 2,000 people were burned at the stake. It is also believed that among these numbers were Protestants, who were true believers. Others were put to death for practicing witchcraft. The inquisitions were finally suppressed in 1834.

Just as in Russia, the land of Spain is defiled through this terrible bloodshed. Prayer teams have been going into Spain to bring healing to the land. The Toward Jerusalem 2 Council, made up of Dan Juster, Don Finto, and John Dawson among others, are just some of those who have prayed over the land. In addition, teams of Spanish intercessors are also rising up in prayer.

Paco Garcia, the coordinator for the Spiritual Warfare Network for Spain, is among those spearheading intercession efforts for Spain. Paco brought teams to the International Congress on Spiritual Warfare in Guatemala in October 1998, where they powerfully repented to all of Latin America and the nations for their horrible abuses during colonial times. Some of the nations that received this repentance included Cuba and the Philippines who were under Spanish rule as well.

The Spanish Slave Trade

The second atrocity that I mentioned earlier is the Spanish

slave trade. The right to a monopoly for supplying African slaves for the Spanish colonies in the Americas was negotiated under what was known as the *asiento de Negros*. Asiento de Negroes means "Negroes contract" in Spanish. This happened between the early 16th and mid-18th centuries. The contractor, or *asentista*, agreed to deliver a stipulated number of male and female slaves for sale in the American markets. Between the years 1600 and 1750 an estimated 450,000 Africans were dispatched to Spanish America under the asiento system.

The atrocities of the slave trade are well known, so I will not document them here. I recently spoke to intercessors from Spain who are making plans for prayer journeys to repent for these terrible sins against the African people.

The Queen of Heaven

We cannot finish this chapter without discussing the serious idolatry that grips Spain through the worship of the Queen of Heaven. I have heard that some cities worship as many as 52 virgins! The oppression for those who try to stand against this spirit is very strong and they are often opposed by the spirit of death who tries to kill those in opposition to the Queen of Heaven. I know that there will be a day when her grip is broken off of this land and the people there will honor Mary, the mother of Jesus, without worshiping the Queen of Heaven. According to Christian and Missionary Alliance statistics, there were 1,109 missionaries to Spain at the time of this writing. However, a number of pastors have told me that the spiritual warfare is so hard on missionaries that each year they receive 1,000 new missionaries, but that 1,000 others choose to leave the country. We need to cry out to God for this land.

Conclusion

While we need to address the strongholds that I have written about in this section on Spain, there are many jewels of delight to be released in this nation as well. For instance, Cadiz, which is very close to the city Paco Garcia comes from and is the birthplace of my son-in-law, is the place where the biblical ships of Tarshish (Is. 60:9) were built. There is much treasure in this beautiful nation, and God has many redemptive purposes for it. Please continue to lift Spain before God so that we will see His Kingdom come and His will done in this strategic land.

For information on church planting in Spain contact Gerry and Marilyn Hartman at P. O. Box 4120 Bethlehem, PA 18018-0120; email at mhartsl29@aol.com. Paco Garcia can be reached by email at nuevavida@inpacto.com, and the Guatemala office can be contacted through Harold Caballeros and Oscar Benitez at El Shaddai, Section 98, P.O. Box 02-5289, Miami, FL 33102.

Notes

1. For this and other statistics on Russia, log onto the Christian & Missionary Alliance's web site at www.cmalliance.or/missions/statistics/russia.htm.
2. Taken from www.britannica.com article on "pogrom."
3. Notes taken from article by Patrick Goodenough.

CHAPTER SEVEN

THE IMPORTANCE
OF EUROPE

by Roger Mitchell

Roger Mitchell and his wife, Sue, live in the United Kingdom and lead Passion, a ministry focusing on reconciliation ministry and city-reaching strategies. Passion exists to affirm and develop these initiatives and to help facilitate the new expressions of church and mission that will result. In addition, Roger is the coordinator of the Spiritual Warfare Network for Europe and is a member of the Board of the International Reconciliation Coalition. Roger and Sue are also part of a team planting a new local church in Camden Town, North London.

Throughout the last decade Europe has been inundated by teams of leaders and intercessors from countries who regard themselves as the children of European empire and mission. These visitors are from the nations of South America, Africa, and Asia. Often with tears and at considerable personal cost, they invariably tell us that they have come to say thank you for the gospel, that there is about to be a revival in Europe, and that they have come to help with the ensuing harvest.

The hearts of the children are turning to the fathers and we Europeans need to make sure that the hearts of the fathers are turning to the hearts of our children (their terminology, not mine). There are two crucial ways that this must happen. Firstly we need to recognize and repent of the sins of Europe, and secondly we need to reveal and overcome the spiritual strongholds that have been built up by our corporate sins and deal with the spiritual powers that inhabit them. This is our apostolic and prophetic task if we are to prepare the way of the Lord for a new era of the gospel in our continent.

The Sins of the "Fathers"

Over the last few years intercession leaders have been trying to uncover Europe's sin, and a clear pattern is beginning to emerge. While I have drawn on the work of several of these, the following list is my attempt to arrive at a comprehensive overview. I make no claim for it to be either final or exhaustive.

1. We have oppressed and divided the church.

Instead of the radical and servant leadership Jesus gave us, we have allowed a controlling imperial spirit to enter the church. This is particularly obvious from the conversion of the Roman Emperor Constantine in the 4th century. In the 4th century we refused the right of the Jewish church to exist with its own distinctives and culture. In the 10th century we split the church between the Orthodox in the East and the

Roman Catholic in the West. In the 16th century we split between Catholic and Protestant, in the 18th century between traditional and nonconformist, and in the 20th century between Pentecostal, charismatic, and Evangelical to name but the most obvious. There is nothing wrong with cultural differences among Christians, or with differences of doctrine or family ways. What is wrong is division: brothers hating brothers; fathers not allowing their spiritual sons to rise; and sons separating from fathers without forgiveness or reconciliation. The fact that Jesus prophesied that it would happen does not make it right and it must be repented of.

2. We have rejected the Jews.

Since the time of the Nicene Council in the 4th century we have refused the right of the Messianic church to exist, insisting that Jewish converts live as Gentiles until the 20th century. We have rejected and ruthlessly persecuted and massacred the Jews for rejecting the Messiah, even though they are our spiritual fathers and Jesus and all the early church founding fathers were Jews.

3. We have exchanged spiritual authority for the secular.

With the conversion of national and political leaders we have repeatedly exchanged spiritual authority for the secular and used national government, legislation, and military might to oppose fellow Christians. We have used secular power in crusades against Jews and Muslims and in religious wars with our fellow European nations.

4. We have given birth to and encouraged humanism in its various forms.

The controlling spirit of the medieval church was partially broken by reformation and renaissance, which allowed the Word and Spirit to break forth. While that was good, it also gave rise to idolatry and humanism. The rise of Socialism and Capitalism lead to the oppression and bondage of millions of the world's people. It has also given rise in recent years to a huge loss of sexual identity and increase in homosexuality, inevitable when we worship and serve the creature rather than the creator, as Paul makes so clear in Romans 1.

5. We have carried out the aggressive colonization of the world.

Since the 16th century we have stolen lands, massacred peoples, and embarked on a policy of grossly unjust trade. While the colonization has stopped, we have continued to behave with racially superior attitudes, a will to rule, and an exclusive spirit towards non-European nations.

6. We have sacrificed our children on the altars of our national pride.

This tendency came to a head with the First World War when the people of Europe were ready and willing to sacrifice thirteen million of their children on the altars of their national pride. It is not enough to say that many of those children gave themselves willingly, or that their loss broke many parents' hearts. Second Kings 3:26-27 shows the consequences of these actions. Great spiritual power is released against God's people and His Kingdom. This is precisely what happened in the ensuing years of the 20th century, including the demonic stronghold of Nazism, which grew up in the wounds of postwar Germany and resulted in the genocide of some six million Jews.

7. We have become the seedbed of modern witchcraft

We have been the birthing ground of modern Freemasonry throughout the world. Drawing as it does from ancient idolatry and occultism, Masonry has played a huge part in the unjust trade of the European colonial era and the imperial wars that have been fought to defend it. All over Europe our church buildings and municipal squares from city to village are polluted by thinly disguised obelisks and shrines replete with Masonic and spiritistic imagery rooted in ancient idolatry and witchcraft which draw occult power from the sacrifice and bloodshed of a century of worldwide European-initiated wars. More recently the witchcraft has manifest in the so-called New Age markets and artifacts and the resurgence of interest in the ancient witchcraft of pre-Christian Europe.

These sins must be explored and acknowledged and humbly repented of by Europeans as the Lord continues to show us how. The fathers of Israel at the times of the restoration following the captivity are the biblical source and inspiration that we need. Daniel and Nehemiah are two who show the way clearly. "O Lord, to us belongs shame of face, to our kings, our princes, and our fathers, because we have sinned against You" (Dan 9:8). "Both my father's house and I have sinned. We have acted very corruptly against You" (Neh. 1:6-7).

Sins Form Strongholds

It is a biblical principle that individual sin that is not repented of leads to demonization. Judas Iscariot is the obvious example of this. He is first described as a thief. When his thieving continues, Satan goes about putting it into his heart to betray Jesus (see John 13:2). Later it is recorded that Satan entered him. What happened next describes the process of corporate sin and demonization and illustrates how demonic strongholds are formed in a city or nation, or for our purposes here, a continent. Judas goes out and conspires with leaders of the Jews who had already found one another, being drawn together by their greed for political power, status, and money. Now they join forces with Judas and form a stronghold which is used by Satan for the arrest, unjust trial, and crucifixion of Jesus.

These sins of Europe that we have outlined began with individual sins of our European fathers, but formed into strongholds which Satan and his hosts have used as a power base against the kingdom of God. It is important for us to understand what these powers are in order to discover them and disempower them. This is the goal of the Spiritual Warfare Network. It is our contention that the powers inhabiting the strongholds of Europe are, in significant part, most usefully understood and described in terms of the Queen of Heaven and the Jezebel spirit. We shall now attempt to understand these powers and how they come to be in such a controlling position in our continent.

Blood That Pollutes and Blood That Fertilizes

After the fall, the first recorded sin was the murder of Abel by his brother, Cain. This sin was rooted in jealousy. Cain was jealous of his brother's sacrifice. Abel's sacrifice was to worship God and cover sin, whereas Cain wished to show off and glorify himself. Instead of accepting correction Cain murdered Abel. God told Cain, "The voice of your brother's blood cries out to Me from the ground. So now you are cursed from the earth, which has opened its mouth to receive your brother's blood from your hand" (Gen 4:10-11).

Cain declared this consequence too hard to bear and instead of becoming a "wanderer on the earth," which God had decreed to limit the effects of the curse, he decided to leave the presence of God and build the first recorded city. His descendant Lamech compounded Cain's sin by turning it into what was viewed as a positive value, "For I have killed a man for wounding me, even a young man for hurting me" (Gen 4:23). In this way, fallen civilization came into being. Before long the sacrifice of humans was seen as one of the greatest values, a means not of polluting the ground and bringing a curse on those who did it, but rather a means of fertilizing the ground and securing blessing for those who did it.

This complete reversal of God's way and intention soon became the basis of a humanistic religion which spread throughout all human civilization which chose to be away from the presence of God. The archetypical myth was of a goddess falling in love with a man who was sacrificed in order to come back as her son. The bloodshed blesses the ground and the mother and child become the objects of worship and the occasion of further sacrifice.

These motifs of goddess worship and human sacrifice formed the basis of the religions of the world's empires: Isis and Osiris in Egypt; Artemis in Greece; Minerva in Rome. After the advent of the gospel in Europe these transformed into Mary and later Britannia. The most common title for this deity is the Queen of Heaven.

In the Bible the effects of individual sin, when not repented of, is demonization. When this continues to be reinforced by wrong choices it creates a corporate agreement or stronghold. This in turn becomes the habitation of demonic power. These powers operate under prince demons or archdemons, like archangels. It is our conviction that such is the case here, and that the Queen of Heaven describes an actual spiritual entity. This is born out by biblical references to her in Jeremiah 7:6 and 44:18-19.

Blood That Cleanses

The way back to the presence of God was the way that Abel had come in the first place, where sacrifice was a gift to cover sin, where the animal was an intercessory offering bridging the gap between humans and God, incarnating the cost of sin to both God and people, and cleansing the effects of the curse caused by the fall. Jesus came to be the fulfillment of this partial offering and interceded for all of humanity once and for all on the cross. His blood cleanses.

However this message was often subverted in Europe once Christianity became the religion of the Roman Empire after the conversion of Constantine in the 4th century. The worship of Mary, or the personification of the state then legitimized by religious expressions of Christianity in the example of Britannia of the British Empire, all too often became the rule of the day.

Goddess Worship
and Human Sacrifice

Throughout the history of European evangelization over the centuries these two streams have interfaced with each other: The worship of the living God and the preaching of Christ's sacrifice at Calvary with some form of goddess worship and the sacrifice of humans, particularly in war. These two streams came to a head at the beginning of the 20th century when the fathers of Europe had the opportunity to choose between the spread of the gospel and the pride of empire. The two greatest missionary nations at the time, Britain and Germany, chose the latter and plunged Europe into a bloodbath of sacrifice in which 13 million children of Europe were sacrificed on the altars of imperial pride, as I mentioned before.

One of the greatest influences in this decision was Freemasonry, which reenacts the ancient sacrifice motifs in its initiation rites. That Freemasonry understood the implications of these decisions is apparent in the many Masonic shrines and memorials that subsequently offered these sacrifices to the sun gods and goddesses through the symbolism of Masonic signs and artifacts.

The linkage of war and empire to the worship of the goddesses of sun and moon or their various transformations is seen in the correlation in Britain of the Roman invasion and the first appearance of the Britannia image in the form of Minerva the Roman goddess of war. Then again, the first apparition of the so-called Virgin Mary at Walsingham occurred at the time of the Norman Conquest. This resulted in Walsingham becoming one of the three great pilgrimage sites in Europe for the next 500 years (the other two were Rome and Santiago de Compostela). The Shrine at Walsingham was destroyed at the time of the reformation. However, the supposed virgin reappeared in 1921 after the end of the First World War, and the shrine was soon reestablished. Today this is an Anglo-Catholic shrine to the Queen of Heaven.

It's probably important at this point to consider the implications of the worship of the Queen of Heaven within the church and how we should regard those churches in that condition of idolatry. I suggest we can get help from the Old Testament Scriptures here, and that the position of the Northern Kingdom of Israel provides a helpful parallel. Neither God nor His prophets gave up easily on the North but rather prayed and prophesied and worked for repentance and reform for as long as possible. So should we. We must be careful not to take an arrogant position, remembering that the southern kingdom of Judah repeatedly fell into the same sins.

The Queen of Heaven and Jezebel

There are three specific biblical instances that provide a framework for understanding the shape of the spiritual powers of Europe.

1.   Jesus speaks clearly about the necessity of first binding the strongman before we can take away his goods (see Matt 12:28-29). Our expectations are, therefore, that we will be able to identify this strongman of Europe.

2.   Revelation 2 and 3 record seven cities and Jesus' words to them. These cities are highly significant for us because they are gateway cities for the gospel into Europe, which, of course, became the launching pad for the gospel into much of the rest of the Gentile world. Therefore the progress of the gospel in those gateway cities is very important to understand. It is clear that there were three particular strongholds emerging in those gates: The Nicolaitans; Balaam; and Jezebel.

It is highly illuminating to notice that the Nicolaitans were the people conquerors (nico from the Greek word *nikao*, meaning to conquer, and lai from *laos*, meaning people). Balaam led the people into idolatry with the gods of Moab, who were a classic manifestation of the male-female coalition involving sacrifice to the Queen of Heaven (see 2 Kings 3 above, and below). Jezebel provided the power base of control from which the Nicolaitan spirit could operate in leading the people to worship the Queen of Heaven. The fact that neither those cities nor their churches exist today strongly suggests that those powers triumphed over the church and once again invaded the European continent—combining forces with the earlier strongholds of their power in pre-Christian days. The Old Testament clearly associates the worship of the Queen of Heaven with the judgment and captivity that came on Israel (see Jer. 7:17-20 and 44:18-23).

3. The prophecy of Zechariah is particularly helpful as it is clearly a handbook for apostolic and prophetic intercession, starting as it does with the vision of the angelic watchers (Chapter 1), followed by the encouragement for the rising generation that the Lord can and will save the city and rebuild it (Chapter 2), and demonstrating the need for identificational repentance and the work of the Holy Spirit (Chapters 3-4). This is then followed by a highly significant vision for our purposes in which "wickedness" in the form of a feminine spirit is manifest and enthroned in Shinar (Babel/Babylon) with the assistance of two more feminine spirits.

This highly important revelation of the shape of the powers that oppose the Spirit of God and the kingdom of God, suggests that the kingdom of darkness manifests in an imperial spirit vaunting itself against God through the ministrations of two feminine spirits. I suggest that in line with the shape of the strongholds manifest in the gateway cities above, that these are the Queen of Heaven and Jezebel, who provide the earthly power base for the former.

It is important to note at this point that the feminine nature of these three manifestations of darkness has nothing negative to say about the female sex! The Creation mandate of Genesis 1:26-28 makes clear that the male aspect emphasizes the taking of dominion whereas the female emphasizes the consolidation and multiplication of that dominion. Hence the portrayal of the kingdom of darkness in feminine form is indicating the stronghold of its settled imperial power, just as the new Jerusalem and the kingdom of God in Revelation is described in feminine terms.

It is our contention that the sins of Europe gave place to these combined powers of the Queen of Heaven and the Jezebel spirit which work to elevate the power of Satan in the nations of the continent of Europe today. We can and must expose them and overcome them if we are going to see the breakthrough in the re-evangelization of Europe that God is calling us to today.

———◆———

CHAPTER EIGHT

THE SWORD IS COMING!

by Martha Lucia

Martha Lucia is the intercessory prayer team leader for Christian International Ministries Network under Bishop Bill Hamon. She is an anointed intercessor and gifted teacher who specializes in helping God's people develop effective prayer lives. In addition, Martha is on the Eagles of God team, under the direction of Chuck Pierce, and travels internationally on various prayer journeys.

————————

I stood in our war room at Christian International agonizing in prayer over the expansive world map that sprawled over an entire wall. I had been here many times before interceding for the billions of helpless and hopeless souls that lived in the dark and desolate part of the world we had come to know as the 10/40 Window. So many living desperate, fruitless lives! So many dying without Jesus! Yet in the midst of it all, we had seen so many miracles over the years as the Body of Christ focused our prayers on this needy land. There was so much to praise God for, as His light had become more and more visible in recent times. And once again I had come to pray and ask that His light would shine even brighter.

That is when it happened. That is when I heard the voice of God say, "Shift your focus! Look at the 40/70 Window!" With those words my eyes looked up and fell on the 40th parallel. As I stared at that line, I could see warring demons standing poised with territorial authority to begin an assault. Then the Lord said to me, "These warring demons are ready to start a new war. You've done the warfare over the 10/40 Window, but if these warring demons can start the war that they have strategized and planned, then the spread of the gospel will be dramatically slowed in the 10/40 Window."

World War III

In 1992, Bishop Bill Hamon, founder of Christian International and a widely respected modern-day prophetic voice, prophesied that Satan had planned a Third World War. In part he prophesied, "I saw the evil spirit that has arisen every so often in men and nations which have Satan's ambition to overcome every nation and rule the world. ...It will become known as the East-West War. [The Eastern Allies'] goal is to overthrow the European Common Market nations and then take over America and the rest of the world.

"...Multimillions will die in this coming war, including thousands in America. Nothing can be done by the politicians to stop this war. ...If we win the war in the spirit realm against the principalities and powers that are motivating the Eastern Allies, then it will not have to be fought in the natural. ...What the Church of Jesus Christ does is the determining factor.

"…The war will be fought and won. It will either be accomplished through supernatural warfare by the Church Army of the Lord, or by the natural armies of the East and West, or by a combination of both. It is all based upon whether a sufficient number of Christians respond properly to take appropriate, aggressive action. The Church must aggressively go on the offensive with revelation knowledge concerning what to do to stop the plans of the enemy. We do not have to stay passive with a 'wait and see' attitude or a doom and gloom perspective that it is all predestined to happen and there is nothing we can do about it. Let us pray that the Church around the world will arise and become the Militant Spiritual Army of the Lord for the sake of our Savior, our children, and our nation."[1]

My primary gifting is what I would describe as a watchman/prophet. I am also a prayer warrior. As such, I tend to look at what the Lord wants to accomplish and ask Him, "What is the warfare that will be necessary to see Your will be done?" When I heard God say it was time to shift our focus to the 40/70 Window, I immediately remembered Bill Hamon's prophecy. As I pondered his words, it became clear to me that the warring demons that I saw sitting on the 40th parallel were, in fact, the very demons who have been charged with stirring up this World War.

I realized that now is the time for the church to rise up to avert the terrible bloodshed this war would produce; and the strategy necessary to accomplish that is to focus on defeating the warring demons of the 40/70 Window!

The Demonic Strategy

By now you may be wondering why Satan would be interested in starting such a war. Beyond the obvious grief and human suffering that would bring great pleasure to the enemy, there is a spiritual strategy behind such a move. Matthew 24:14 says, "And this gospel of the kingdom will be preached in all the world as a witness to all the nations, and then the end will come."

Can Satan stop the end from coming? No. Revelation 20:10 says, "The devil, who deceived them, was cast into the lake of fire and brimstone where the beast and the false prophet are. And they will be tormented day and night forever and ever." Can Satan stop his prophesied judgment from coming to pass? Absolutely not!

There is a chance, however, that if Satan can orchestrate a war, he may be able to extend his time as ruler of this world. The thinking is simple. During times of war, all else comes to a halt. Such a war would block or severely deter the entrance of the gospel into the 10/40 Window region simply because nations that are at war strictly limit those who are allowed in. In addition, history shows that nations at war move to expel any non-nationals that they consider suspicious, which often include Christian workers and missionaries. If Satan can stop the flow of the gospel, even for a season, his own time may be extended. History shows time and time again that enemies from the north attack and oppress those in the south. It would, therefore, make sense that the spiritual, and even physical, aggression would begin in the 40/70 Window to oppress the move of God in the 10/40 Window.

Warring Demons

There is a hierarchy of principalities and powers already firmly established who, as we will discuss shortly, have stirred great wars in the earth from the 40/70 Window. The Queen of Heaven, under various adaptive forms, is at the top of the demonic structure. Through the adaptation of the Virgin Mary, she controlled much of the British Empire, which conquered through war and bloodshed. Through the adaptation of the Moon Goddess, many Muslim jihads, or holy wars, have taken place. In addition, many conquering warrior tribes, including the Scythians, Alans, Huns, and Kyazars, worshiped a "Divine Mother."

In addition to the Queen of Heaven, other high-ranking territorial spirits of the area are ones whose assignment is to create terror, depression, grief, heaviness, failure, and intoxications. The very spirit of the future Antichrist, a spirit known as Gog, may come from these territorial spirits. Ezekiel prophesied against Gog and his warring cohorts strongly throughout Ezekiel 38 and 39. Ezekiel begins the decree of judgment against this spirit by saying:

"Now the word of the LORD came to me, saying, 'Son of man, set your face against Gog, of the land of Magog, the prince of Rosh, Meshech, and Tubal, and prophesy against him, and say, 'Thus says the Lord GOD: 'Behold, I am against you, O Gog, the prince of Rosh, Meshech, and Tubal. I will turn you around, put hooks into your jaws, and lead you out, with all your army, horses, and horsemen, all splendidly clothed, a great company with bucklers and shields, all of them handling swords''''" (Ezek. 38:1-4).

The names of Gog's confederates, listed in Ezekiel 38, can be identified as peoples who lived in the mountainous area southeast of the Black Sea and southwest of the Caspian, currently in central Turkey. This is of particular significance because Turkey is considered, both physically and spiritually, to be the hinge nation between the 10/40 and the 40/70 Windows. The principalities and powers behind these warring peoples, and against whom God has set His face are, therefore, chief spirits in the 40/70 Window region. As we study these spirits' names throughout the Bible, we can begin to see what strongholds Satan has that we are called to war against. Let's look at a few Scriptures that name these spirits:

"Javan, Tubal, and Meshech were your traders. They bartered human lives and vessels of bronze for your merchandise" (Ezek. 27:13).

"There are Meshech and Tubal and all their multitudes, with all their graves around it, all of them uncircumcised, slain by the sword, though they caused their terror in the land of the living" (Ezek. 32:26).

"Woe is me, that I dwell in Meshech, that I dwell among the tents of Kedar! My soul has dwelt too long with one who hates peace. I am for peace; but when I speak, they are for war" (Ps. 120:5-7).

"Now when the thousand years have expired, Satan will be released from his prison and will go out to deceive the nations which are in the four corners of the earth, Gog and Magog, to gather them together to battle, whose number is as the sand of the sea" (Rev. 20:7-8).

These are warring spirits who continually stir up war in order to barter with the souls of human beings. They are, in effect, slave traders or traffickers in the human soul. The spirits keep people in bondage as prisoners of war between the kingdom of darkness and the kingdom of light. By continually stirring up war in the natural realm, these territorial spirits are able to enslave the peoples of the region.

Another reason these spirits long to stir up war prematurely is because Ezekiel 36 and 37 speak of the restoration of the land and the people of Israel. Chapter 38 says that Gog will come against a restored Israel. By stirring up wars and keeping Israel from coming into a state of restoration, these spirits may also be able to stave off the judgments prophesied in Ezekiel 38 for a period of time (although not forever).

If you believe the Great Commission to be our principal assignment from God, then it is easy to see why we are at conflict with these spirits in particular. Our call is to set the captives free by escorting them from Satan's grip into God's Kingdom. We are, therefore, in direct conflict with these spirits of the 40/70 Window.

What History Reveals

In shifting our focus toward the 40/70 Window, we must confront the fact that warring spirits from this region have left their mark on the land throughout human history in war after war, in the creation of major nuclear forces, and in the formation of political and religious strongholds.

Many of the earth's major wars have begun in this region as these warring demons have locked their power into the lives of such men as Alexander the Great, Kublai Khan, Genghis Khan, Peter the Great, Napoleon, Hitler, and Stalin, to name just a few. In addition, many of the world's conquering empires had their roots in the 40/70 Window, including the Roman Empire, the Ottoman Empire, the British Empire, and the Soviet Union. Certain philosophies contrary to God's Word, including humanism and Communism, were also birthed in this region.

Mobilizing the demonic hierarchy of this region for war is nothing new for Satan. He has done it for millennia. He is again stirring these powers to war. But this time, the Lord is preparing a mighty army of warriors to defeat Satan's plan and advance the gospel of Jesus Christ as never before. That is why God is shifting our focus to the 40/70 Window.

Apostolic Intercession

Throughout the decade of the '90s, God taught us a great deal about spiritual warfare and how to war in the heavenlies. Peter Wagner focused so well on this in the first chapters of this book. He also pointed out the important lessons the Lord has been teaching us about prophetic intercession. I do not believe that we will be able to accomplish all we need to without understanding prophetic intercession and prophetic acts, and the important role they play in warfare.

In addition to the realm of prophetic intercession, I believe the Lord is teaching His Body about another new level of warfare that I call apostolic intercession. I have heard Chuck Pierce refer to this as "legislative praying." This type of warfare prayer is decreed with such power that the earth and its people must respond. They must line up with God and His purposes.

It would seem that only God Himself could have this kind of power to speak into the earth, but there are times that He chooses His saints to speak forth in apostolic intercession. A biblical example of this is when Elijah prayed in such a way that the very atmosphere responded by producing a great drought. It took another such prayer to end the drought.

This is the kind of prayer that allows us to do greater works than even Jesus did when He was on earth. Jesus says to us, "Most assuredly, I say to you, he who believes in Me, the works that I do he will do also; and greater works than these he will do, because I go to My Father. And whatever you ask in My name, that I will do, that the Father may be glorified in the Son. If you ask anything in My name, I will do it" (John 14:12-14).

Apostolic intercession is the kind of prayer that will avert a demonically planned World War. It is the kind of prayer that we need to battle in the 40/70 Window. It is the kind of prayer that will change the world!

A New Position

How do we become the kind of intercessors that have the power to pray apostolically? We must begin to pray from a new position, seated in the heavenlies with God Himself. Ephesians 2:4-6 says, "But God, who is rich in mercy, because of His great love with which He loved us, even when we were dead in trespasses, made us alive together with Christ (by grace you have been saved), and raised us up together, and made us sit together in the heavenly places in Christ Jesus."

The only way that we can come into that new position is through redemption of the soul and death to self! When our soul is redeemed, our spirit is raised up in resurrection life and seated in heavenly places with Christ. But we cannot be raised into that new position until we have died to ourselves. That is a choice we must make beyond salvation. We must choose to live lives full of holiness and sacrifice before the Lord, preferring His will above our own. It is then that we can come into a place of intercession seated beside Him.

It is only from that position that we have the kind of power to pray apostolically, because it is only from that position that we are close enough to the Father to know what we should be praying. If we are at the right hand of the Father and participating in what Jesus is praying, we will know what has been bound and loosed in heaven, and we can then declare a thing and see it happen on earth. That is the essence of apostolic praying.

When we come into that place in Christ, seated with Him,

we can see the world as He sees the world, and we will know what we have been sent to do. Because of our position with the Father, we will be able to pray, speak, proclaim, declare, and release those things that God has already loosed in the heavens into the earth and see the world changed! But, as Marty Cassady tells us in her chapter, it will require a new level of commitment and a new level of holiness to enter into this the new level of apostolic praying that it will take to see God's purposes accomplished in the 40/70 Window.

The sword is coming one way or another! But if we will align ourselves in heavenly places and fight the war in the spirit, then the sword will not come to kill millions, as is Satan's plan, but will come to break free countless multitudes of prisoners of war held captive in the kingdom of darkness!

Notes

1. Taken from a fax from Bill Hamon's office to *Charisma* magazine, dated August 5, 1996.

—————◆—————

CHAPTER NINE

Joining Heaven and Earth in Praying for the 40/70 Window

by Marty Cassady

Marty Cassady is an ordained minister who serves as the Executive Secretary of Global Harvest Ministries under Peter and Doris Wagner. With a heart of intercession toward the nations, Marty frequently participates as an intercessor and prayer leader in prayer rooms at international conferences. She is a member of the Eagles of God team under the direction of Chuck Pierce, and has often traveled to the 40/70 Window and throughout the world to minister on prayer journeys..

—————————

Is *That* Really Luxury?

The western world, especially the United States, has become a push-button society. We push a button to wash our dishes, to withdraw cash from the ATM, to cook our food, to operate our automobiles, and to entertain ourselves as we sit in front of a large screen television.

But have we, as those called to pray for nations, seriously considered the price we may be paying for all of this "luxury"? In a society where luxury is commonplace, even though many times we don't identify it as luxury, we have become anesthetized to the effects of how we live our everyday lives.

I'm not suggesting that these things are wrong in and of themselves. But I am suggesting that we need to search ourselves and know to what degree we would be willing to "go and sell all" if the Lord requires that of us. Would we be willing to give up our lifestyle full of luxury to follow the Lord's call to pray for the nations?

A Commercial Babylon

As we begin to seek the agreement of heaven and earth in prayer for the 40/70 Window, we, especially those of us who are Westerners, must take serious and careful consideration of how we relate spiritually to the luxuries that surround us. We, therefore, must come to understand how the enemy can use a lifestyle of instant gratification and comfort to create a "commercial Babylon" within our society and within our hearts.

Biblically, Babylon represents a world in rebellion against God. In Revelation 17 and 18 we find Babylon depicted as a prostitute who is luring people away from the gospel through her glamour.

• Revelation 18: 4-5 says, "Come out of her, my people, so that you will not share in her sins, so that you will not receive any of her plagues; for her sins are piled up to heaven and God has remembered her crimes."

• Revelation 18: 11 says, "The merchants of the earth will

weep and mourn over her because no one buys their cargoes any more."

The "her" spoken of here, I believe, refers to a commercial Babylon. We are given a picture of the merchants of the earth in mourning because their commerce has been stopped. This commercial Babylon can be compared to a religious Babylon. Both the religious Babylon spoken of in Revelation 17 and the Commercial Babylon, as represented in Revelation 18, commit fornication with the kings of the earth and there are many similarities between the two.

But, as Gordon Lindsey outlines in his booklet, *The Two Babylons*, "Closer examination [of Revelation 17 and 18] shows that there are also many points of irreconcilable contrasts which make it practically impossible to identify the two as the same Babylon."[1]

Lindsay goes on to list several contrasts, a few of which are:

"No merchants are enriched by the commerce of the first, while there are of the second (Rev. 18:19).

"Men do not stand afar off for fear of destruction in the case of one, but they do of the other (Rev. 18:8).

"Merchandise is not described in the first. It is of the second.

"A period of time is required for the destruction of the first, which involves the co-operation of the ten kingdoms (Rev 17:16).

"In the second, the destruction took place in one day (Rev. 18:10)."[2]

Set Apart

Jesus warned us of serving two masters in Luke 16:13, "No

servant can serve two masters; for either he will hate the one and love the other, or else he will be loyal to the one and despise the other. You cannot serve God and mammon."

Why am I going into the whole issue of a commercial Babylon? Because for us to enter into the warfare for the 40/70 Window, we must be sure that we are not held captive in either the religious or the commercial Babylon. Both of these strongholds are represented in the 40/70 countries. One of the religious strongholds of the world is Rome, and the thinking of London and Switzerland is synonymous with thinking of great wealth. If we enter into the warfare for the 40/70 Window without having dealt with these potential strongholds in ourselves, we are open to a great attack from the enemy!

Over and over we see examples in God's Word that admonish His people to keep themselves "set apart" from the false gods and from the customs of idolatrous people or nations. To avoid casualties we must not enter into warfare over the 40/70 Window without first taking a look at ourselves and asking the Lord to show us where we have become vulnerable to these Babylonian systems.

How many of us have asked the Lord to show us how we are held captive to the spirit of mammon or the luxuries of life? Have we sought the Lord's revelation over the strongholds in our minds and can we truly say we are free from religious spirits?

If you feel that you are being called to do warfare in this arena, please be sure to spend some time with the Lord seeking revelation over any connection you may have in either the religious or commercial Babylon.

Where Are Our Roots?

As we begin to search ourselves before the Lord, we must remember that for many of us in the United States our ancestry can be traced back to the countries of the 40/70 Window. Because certain generational iniquities may have crossed the ocean with our forefathers, we are susceptible to having those same strongholds within us. The battle over the 10/40 Window was not as personal for us because it centered around overt idolatry, which those of us in the West are not as likely to be involved in. Yes, we have our idols, but overt idolatrous worship is not part of the norm for us.

It is a different story with the 40/70 Window. Our roots go back to many of the religious spirits that are entrenched in the 40/70 Window. How many of us come from denominational backgrounds birthed in the Protestant Reformation or from the Catholic Church? It is difficult to talk about the "religious spirits" that we will be dealing with in the 40/70 Window without mentioning how those spirits relate to the "intellectual spirit" that I will be calling the "Prince of Greece."

The Prince of Greece: A Religious Spirit

The United States is strongly influenced by the intellectual presumption of humanistic thinking that is also known as the Prince of Greece. This is the spirit behind the "program-seminar" thinking that many churches are using today. It is secular humanism at its very best, but leaves no room at all for a move of Holy Spirit. When the perfect-to-the-minute plans of these seminar-type institutions are interfered with, you will see the spirit of religion raise its head.

This intellectual mind-controlling spirit is referred to in 2 Timothy 4:3-4 where Paul shares with Timothy that, "The time will come when they will not endure sound doctrine, but according to their own desires, because they have itching ears, they will heap up for themselves teachers; and they will turn their ears away from the truth, and be turned aside to fables."

In his book, *Apostolic Strategies Affecting Nations*, Dr. Jonathan David writes, "The wave of deception, manipulation and witchcraft has already infiltrated the church's life and government. Church splits, liberalism and disunity have taken away the spiritual strength of many churches. The rising of men and women who refuse to change and who will resist any change in the church has become an increasingly important issue. These resisters are not allowing the church to move into the prophetic and apostolic dimensions which God is releasing and restoring today."[3]

The religious spirits that we will need to confront in the 40/70 Window are the same that were entrenched during the time of Jesus' ministry here on earth, and are also entrenched in much of American Christianity. They are ritualistic, legalistic, and always ready to accuse and destroy anything that raises a voice against them. Much of their power is in the "form" that is used for worship and when that "form" is tampered with, they let everyone know about it. Comments like:

"Why would we sing the same line over and over again?"

"Whatever happened to the way we used to do it?"

"Tongues and apostles ended when the last of Jesus' apostles died!"

will offer you a clue as to what this religious spirit says.

Just as we must deal with the Babylonian issues of our hearts, we must also deal with the thinking brought on by the religious spirits of the Prince of Greece.

Focus To Overcome

After Celebration Ephesus, Peter Wagner announced that the focus for our ministry would shift to the 40/70 Window. I then began to seek the Lord for His strategy for this new mission. Holy Spirit spoke very clearly to me that the warfare of the future would not look like the warfare of the past. Strategies we had used in the past would not overthrow the powers that He would ask us to go against in the future.

He said, "Marty, you have warred in the past based on the power of the blood of Jesus and the Word of the Lord, but in the future My heart's desire is for you to war with more of an agreement between heaven and earth. I want to show you how to call the agreement of My power in the heavens and the power that is resident on the earth through My Holy Spirit's indwelling in the saints. The power of the blood and the Word, and the weapons I have given you will not be diminished. But I want more, much more from you."

In the following weeks, as I sought more revelation on what the Lord had spoken to me. God began to lead me to Scripture that showed me His desire for this agreement of heaven and earth to become more balanced. The strategy was going to be one that would require those of us involved in this battle to die to ourselves and to our desires and to die to the need for luxuries in ways that we had not seen before.

Jesus Himself taught His disciples in John 12 that unless a seed falls to the earth and dies it would remain a single seed, but in its death it would produce many seeds. He went on to say, "He who loves his life will lose it, and he who hates his life *in this world* will keep it for eternal life" (v. 25, emphasis mine).

John is told in Revelation 12:11 that "*they* overcame [the accuser of the brethren] by the blood of the Lamb and by the word of *their* testimony, and *they* did not love *their* lives to the death" (emphasis mine). When we seek to enter into strategies and battle over nations and continents, more will be required of us. We will have to deal with the mammon in our own hearts, and with religious spirits that have convinced us that there is only one way to "do church." We will have to deal with what is in us to such an extent that we will even face death, if God so requires, to overcome His enemies.

In God's infinite and perfect plan, His will and His heart for us is that we go from glory to glory, to be changed into the image of His Son, and to know that the one who began the work in us will carry it on to completion until the day of Christ Jesus. When Holy Spirit spoke to me and said He wanted more of an agreement between heaven and earth, what became clear was that He wants those of us called to war to become more aware of spiritual forces than we have been in the past.

He wants us to be willing to lay down the things of this world in order to bring about a spiritual force in the heavenlies, an agreement of heaven and earth, using the weapons of our warfare, the blood of the Lamb, and the Word of the Lord, but also to be broken, yielded vessels here on earth that have learned the process of dying to oneself and that, like Jesus, can truly say, "The ruler of this world is coming, and he has nothing in Me" (John 14: 30). That posture before the Lord will give us the focus to overcome to enemies of the 40/70

Window.

God Is Raising Up An Army to Join Heaven and Earth

In a recent memo circulated to several leaders of the worldwide prayer movement and members of the International Spiritual Warfare Network, C. Peter Wagner stated that the countries of the 40/70 Window "cover twelve time zones and encompass the waves of the Atlantic Ocean rolling up through the Bay of Biscay on one side and the waves of the Pacific Ocean through the Bering Sea on the other side."   As well as the geographical distinctions the cultural and political ideologies are every bit as varied.

I believe that much like we see the diversity in the religious, cultural, and political profiles of the 40/70 Window, we will see the diversity of the warriors the Lord will raise up to join in this battle. They will come from different continents, backgrounds, and cultures. But they will all have one thing in common: the willingness to die to self, to die to the need for luxury, and to die to the need for the approval of others. They will be totally sold out to their commitment to the Lord!

From the fire of our circumstances to the brokenness in our lives, the Lord, in His master plan for us, will bring us to the point where we *know* we have heard His call to enter into this war for the nations. This kind of call is not a "gentle whisper" but a forceful knowing that wherever He leads you, will follow.

It will be as if you are wired for warfare. You cannot read the Word without seeing a strategy or a feeling called to war for what is rightfully the Lord's. Your heart beats to see the enemies of the Lord made His footstool (see Luke 20: 42). This is an army that longs to see every tribe and language and people and nation come to saving knowledge of Jesus because, more than anything, this army wants to see Jesus return.

Kjell Sjoberg wrote the following in his powerful book, *The Prophetic Church,* "Paul in Ephesians 4 talks of the building-up of the body of Christ, to bring the people of God to the same spiritual stature as that which Moses and Elijah had when they spoke with Jesus on the mountain of transfiguration. We will grow up into him who is the Head; we will grow to maturity, to the whole measure of the fullness of Christ (Ephesians 4:12-15). When did Elijah and Moses undergo those experiences that enabled them to be partners in conversation with Jesus? Were they before or after Moses' death? Were they before or after Elijah's ascension? They were before, in each case, while they were still on earth. In this way they became men of God. We have transferred too much of our hope over to the other side, and therefore have up to now missed much of the spiritual growth that God has wanted in our lives here and now, while we are on earth. In the darkest times, at the close of this age, Jesus will bring his church into maturity."[4]

I don't know about you, but that last sentence excites me! Jesus is bringing us to maturity here and now and it is for one reason: ministering to the nations that are on His heart! God's army is being called and enabled to fight the good fight to win the nations and continents of the world. But the cost is, as I stated before, dying to oneself.

Regulations for Conquest

In both Exodus 23 and Joshua 23 we see regulations for conquest. In Exodus 23 we see the following orders given:

- An angelic host will lead the way.
- God Himself will wipe out the enemy.
- Do not worship the false gods but destroy them.
- Do not neglect to worship the one true God.
- God will throw the enemy's camp into confusion.
- Then all the enemies will turn their backs and run.

In Joshua 23 we see:

- Remain strong, obey all that is written in the Book of the Law.
- Do not associate with the enemy nations or invoke the names of their gods.
- Hold fast to the Lord.
- The Lord Himself has driven out the enemy.
- Be careful to love the Lord.

Over and over in both of these chapters we see that it is the Lord God who is in charge of both the strategy for war against the enemy and the way the battle will be waged. We must not move without the strategy of the Lord for the 40/70 Window or without a clear call that we are to join the army!

Timing Is An Issue

I believe that, even as some of you are reading this final chapter, you are asking yourselves if you are to be one of those warriors. I also believe that as you seek the Lord, He will show you where you may be vulnerable. You might want to ask yourself, "If the Lord asked me to give my car away, would I do it?" Are you able to place all of your family members and loved ones totally in His keeping? Is there any portion of the Word of God that you do not really believe?   Have you been tried and tested in the fire of this life and has the Lord spoken personally to you as you have walked through those trials?

Strategic-level spiritual warfare, as Peter Wagner pointed out in Chapter One, is not a "good idea" for everyone reading this book. It is not a higher calling to some than to others, but it is a place for a few who have been tested and who are willing to go where the Lord sends, even though it may be a one-way ticket.

C. Peter Wagner, states in *Confronting The Powers*, "An obvious question arises. Why was it that Paul did not go into the temple of Diana, but John did? The answer is simple, because it rests on a principle I have mentioned several times: *In strategic-level spiritual warfare, proceed only on God's timing.*"[5]

In Judges 7 we have a good example of the Lord eliminating some of Gideon's large army so that Israel would not boast that they had been responsible for winning the battle. The timing for battle is not just an important issue for those who will be leading the assaults, but for each of us as individuals who feel called to this war.

Ask the Lord about the timing issue in your own life. The stakes are very high as we move into the 40/70 Window. The army has been tried and tested through the decade of the '90s. Many have been knit together sovereignly by the Lord, praying for both national and international conferences. Many of you may have even joined in prayer focuses for Operation Ice Castle and Operation Queen's Palace/Celebration Ephesus.

We are now a recognizable army, all to the praise of the Lord. But we are also recognized and hated by the enemy. War often times has casualties and they are unavoidable, but let us not let the "timing" of our going out to war be the cause of a casualty. Seek the leading of Holy Spirit, and when you hear Him say it is time to join the battle of the 40/70 Window, be reminded that He who is within us is greater than he who is within this world!

Notes

1. Gordan Lindsay, *The Two Babylons* (Dallas, TX: Christ for the Nations, Inc., 1988), p. 411.
2. Ibid., pp. 411-412.
3. Johathan David, *Apostolic Strategies Affecting Nations* (No: 4, Taman Mas Ria, Jalan Junid, 84000 Muar, Johor, Malaysia. 1997.) p. 6.
4. Kjell Sjoberg, *The Prophetic Church*, (Chichester, England: New Wine Press, 1992), pp. 32-33.
5. C. Peter Wagner, *Confronting the Powers* (Ventura, CA: Regal Books, 1996), p. 221.

Don't miss the exciting companion to this book!

Confronting the Queen of Heaven
by C. Peter Wagner

This book takes a look at what is perhaps one of the most powerful spirits in Satan's hierarchy: the Queen of Heaven. Throughout history this high-ranking principality has kept countless multitudes of lost souls blinded to the gospel. In *Confronting the Queen of Heaven*, C. Peter Wagner takes a look at how the Queen of Heaven has accomplished her goals in the past, and how she is manifesting in the world today to keep untold numbers in spiritual darkness. Readers of this book will discover how God is mounting an assault against this dark force to see the captives set free!

Paperback • 42p
ISBN 0.9667481.3.1
$6.00

Confronting the Queen of Heaven is available at your local Christian bookstore, or by calling toll-free 1-877-924-6374.